Steam Around the West Midlands

MICHAEL WELCH

Rails

Published by Rails Publishing

Printed by 1010 Printing International Ltd

© Michael Welch 2015
Layout by Michael Welch. Typesetting
and book production by Lucy Frontani.

Front Cover: An unidentified 'King' Class
4-6-0 has just left Snow Hill with a London
express, and gets into its stride past Moor
Street station; this shot was taken in 1962.
Derek Penney

Back Cover: The new Rotunda building, part
of the ill-fated 'Bullring' development, takes
shape in the background as Stanier Class
5MT No.44909 enters Birmingham New
Street station on 15th June 1963.
W. Potter/Kidderminster Railway Museum

Title Page: Ashchurch, seen here on 22nd
July 1961, was an interesting country station
and the junction for the branch lines to
Upton-on-Severn and Evesham.
Charles Firminger

Details of Michael Welch's other
railway titles can be found at
www.capitaltransport.com

The brightly painted station nameboard
at Ashchurch left passengers in no doubt
where they should change if they were
travelling to any of the places indicated.
Some passengers may have got a nasty
shock when they discovered how long they
would have to wait for a connecting train!
Ashchurch became part of the LMR upon
nationalisation in 1948 but was transferred
to the WR from 1st February 1958 and this
probably accounts for the newly repainted
nameboard. Note that the station's name is
also displayed on the gas lamp. This picture
was taken on 13th May 1961. *John Langford*

Introduction

Walsall, Wednesbury, Willenhall and West Bromwich are just a few of the many industrial towns that constitute the West Midlands, the hub being the city of Birmingham which was often referred to as 'the workshop of the world'. In 1907 the goods agent at Curzon Street cited the principal industries in the area as 'hardware, iron, steel, brass, bedsteads plus foodstuff' and noted that there were 1,000 different trades.

The first long distance railway to serve Birmingham was the Grand Junction Railway which opened its 82½ miles-long line from Newton, near Warrington, to a temporary terminus at Vauxhall on 4th July 1837; this was the first of the great trunk routes to be constructed in Great Britain. Less than a year later, on 24th June 1838, the London & Birmingham Railway opened with a limited service, the full timetable being provided from 17th September. The next major development was the arrival in the city of the Birmingham & Gloucester Railway in December 1840, followed in February 1842 by the opening of the Birmingham & Derby Junction Railway's Lawley Street terminus. There was then a lull in the expansion of the main line network until the Oxford, Worcester & Wolverhampton Railway reached Stourbridge in May 1852 (and later Wolverhampton) while a few months afterwards the mixed gauge GWR route from Banbury to Birmingham was brought into use. These lines formed the framework from which the dense tangle of routes serving Birmingham and the surrounding area developed. The Trent Valley Line between Rugby and Stafford, part of, arguably, Great Britain's most important trunk route, skirted the West Midlands and must not be forgotten; this opened in September 1847.

The vast West Midlands conurbation which developed, with its seemingly endless sprawl of factories, steelworks and collieries was, however, home to some particularly fascinating lines, none more so than the idiosyncratic Harborne and Halesowen branches; these were just the kind of byways that makes the study of railways so rewarding. The former, opened in 1874 to serve one of Birmingham's growing suburbs, remained independent until 1922 and during the peak of its popularity had a very intensive service. The latter had opened throughout by September 1883 but the passenger service between Halesowen and Northfield only lasted until April 1919 while that to Old Hill survived until 1927. Workmen's trains to and from Longbridge along the entire length of the route were unaffected by these changes and ran until 1958.

One of the attractions of the railway system in the West Midlands in the twilight of the steam era was the wonderful variety of locomotives that could be observed. Of course, trains to and from New Street were normally the preserve of former LMSR classes while just a few hundred yards away at Snow Hill station there was an altogether different scene with copper-capped former GWR locomotives to the fore. Birmingham was, however, almost unique among British provincial cities because, on rare occasions, representatives from the other pre-nationalisation companies also could be seen. A date that will always be remembered by enthusiasts in the area is 27th April 1963 when Bulleid Pacifics were provided to take Southampton fans to a football match at Villa Park. The consecration of the new Coventry cathedral brought many pilgrims to the city and, during the same month that Birmingham was invaded by Bulleid 4-6-2s, a V2 Class 2-6-2 powered a special from Newcastle upon Tyne and a few days later a B1 Class 4-6-0 also appeared.

During the compilation of this book it has been my aim to illustrate as many West Midlands routes as possible but some were apparently very little photographed in colour; perhaps photographers were deterred due to the very early introduction of diesel units on certain routes in the Birmingham area. By way of compensation I have included some particularly interesting pictures taken on routes that would not normally be regarded as part of the West Midlands network. These include the little-known line that ran northwards from Nuneaton to Moira and Coalville and the scenic backwater from Bewdley to Woofferton Junction through the delightful Wyre Forest.

Compilation of this album has benefited from assistance provided by Bob Dalton, Chris Evans, Dave Fakes, John Langford and Terry Phillips who suggested many amendments and improvements to the text. Pictures from the Bluebell Railway Museum, Kidderminster Railway Museum, R C Riley and Lens of Sutton collections were kindly made available by Tony Hillman, David Postle, Rodney Lissenden and Peter Fidczuk respectively and thanks are offered to those gentlemen. Charles Firminger's slides were provided by Bob Bridger while the luggage labels are from the Les Dench collection.

M.S.W.
Burgess Hill West Sussex
April 2015

Contents

Years after the SMJR passed into history this cast iron relic was still *in situ* at Stratford-upon-Avon. *Gerald Daniels*

A fascinating aerial view, taken on a very gloomy day, of the old New Street station and hinterland as it was in the mid-1950s. The former LNWR side of the station, whose tracks lead into New Street South tunnel (also known as Proof House tunnel), is on the left while on the right are the former MR platforms concealed beneath a curving overall roof. The very tall brick building on the left is the Queen's hotel. The two halves of the station were separated by Queens Drive which was a public right of way; this was partially covered and accommodated a taxi rank. On the left of the photograph is Navigation Street with three bus stops visible while Hill Street runs across the foreground of the picture. Many of the cars depicted, not to mention the vintage Birmingham Corporation buses, would be regarded as museum pieces today. The LNWR's first terminal station in Birmingham was at Curzon Street but this was clearly inadequate and on 3rd August 1846 the company obtained parliamentary approval for an extension to a site in New Street. The Act stipulated that as the station was going to obliterate King Street, one of the city's main thoroughfares, a footpath must run through the station premises. Birmingham councillors voted in favour of New Street which was considered to be more conveniently located for the travelling public, more accessible to local businesses and in an altogether better part of the city centre than the other proposed site at Snow Hill. The extension Act provided the LNWR with a line, engineered by Robert Stephenson, of just under one mile in length at a modest cost of £37,000; the route involved boring a 273 yards-long tunnel. On 1st June 1854 New Street was formally opened and used by the MR for a few local services from 1st July when Curzon Street was closed to regular passenger trains. It should be noted, however, that the MR's Bristol to Derby expresses used the 'direct line' via Camp Hill and did not serve New Street. In 1876 the single track Birmingham West Suburban Railway was opened from Lifford to a terminus in Granville Street on the fringe of the city centre; the local company was soon swallowed up by the MR. In 1881 the MR obtained an Act authorising doubling of the branch and the laying of a connection from Church Road Junction to New Street which involved the boring of three tunnels, one of which passed beneath a canal. The transformation of this relatively quiet suburban branch into a main line railway was a huge civil engineering operation and Joseph Firbank, a renowned railway contractor, was awarded the contract. Work began in 1883 and in October 1885 some MR express trains started to use the new platforms at New Street that had been constructed alongside the LNWR station, the two being separated by the station drive which was a public right of way. Granville Street station was closed but the line serving it was extended to Worcester Wharf (later the Central Goods Depot), opened in 1887. Initially, some MR expresses were routed through the LNWR side of New Street but caused congestion and from 1889 MR traffic was henceforth confined to its own station. On the other side of New Street the MR constructed its own independent, double track access to the station from Landor Street Junction and this was the final operation resulting from the MR's arrival in the city. Operations on both sides of the station were plagued by steep gradients at the approaches; from the east both routes have a nasty patch of 1 in 50, while westbound trains have to contend with climbs at 1 in 77/80, some of which is in a succession of tunnels. The layout of the old station was reasonably straightforward, the LNWR side had four through platforms while the MR part of the station also had four. Operations on the former were, however, handicapped by short platforms: only Platform 3 could take a 15-coach train, while others could accommodate only 10 coaches or less. This meant that trains were often forced to draw up again after stopping at the starting signals to ensure the rear of the train was not fouling entry to another platform. Platform Nos. 1 and 2 were bays used solely by local services. The MR part of New Street station consisted of four through platforms, Nos. 7 to 10, with a little-used bay at the west end. Unfortunately, the station suffered bombing on five occasions during the Second World War which resulted in the all-over glass roof on the LNWR side being totally shattered; it was subsequently removed and replaced by individual platform canopies. While its GWR neighbour was light, clean and airy, dingy and decrepit New Street was a veritable blot on the landscape and in 1964 was described by a local worthy as the worst main line station he had seen in Europe or the United States. The £4,500,000 reconstruction of the station as part of the West Coast Main Line electrification was a massive undertaking and BR trumpeted its role as 'the finest rail inter-change centre in the country' hailing New Street 'as a station befitting the second city'. But the design was a three-tier structure, incorporating a spacious covered shopping centre, beneath which was the concourse, with the artificially lit, narrow platforms at the lowest level. The design created a wind tunnel and passengers almost froze on a cold, windy day and those who had had the displeasure of using the ramshackle, old New Street station in the past probably reflected that the old premises were not that bad after all!
Lens of Sutton Association

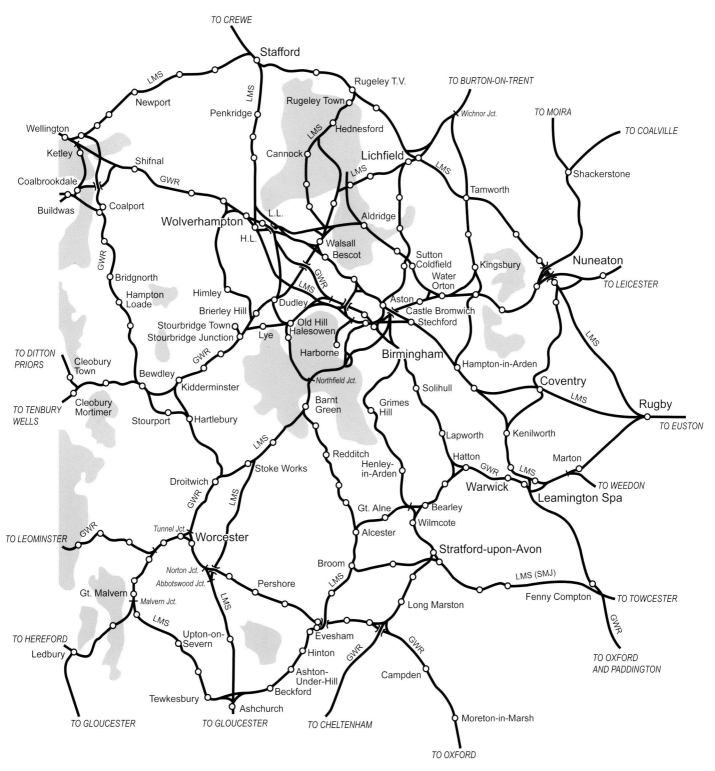

Map of routes in West Midlands and surrounding area
Note that for clarity not all lines are shown

5

In the 1830s the Manchester & Birmingham Railway (MBR) was at war with the neighbouring Grand Junction Railway (GJR) and in 1839 sought a route to London through the Trent Valley that would be independent of its neighbour; the projected course was from Stone to Rugby. This idea failed to get Parliament's approval but the concept of a more direct route from the north west of England and the Potteries to the Capital had caught the imagination of many people. Influential businessmen in Nuneaton, for example, considered that the proposed line, which would permit the much speedier transport of goods than hitherto, would be 'of the greatest advantage to the town'. The GJR was implacably opposed to any scheme for a line through the Trent Valley because it would clearly siphon off its Manchester traffic and that from the Potteries once railways became established in that area. However, when the Trent Valley line was authorised by an Act of 1845 the GJR subscribed much of the capital and obtained full running powers over the line – in effect, the best of both worlds. The first sod was cut by the Prime Minister, Sir Robert Peel, the MP for Tamworth, in November 1845 and the largest engineering work was Shugborough tunnel (777 yards long). A grand banquet was organised to mark the opening of the line but, alas, problems arose at the last minute due to concern about the cast iron bridges following the collapse of a similar structure across the river Dee at Chester and the opening was deferred. In the event the banquet took place as scheduled but there was a considerable delay before the first trains ran on 15th September 1847 and one of the country's most strategically important lines was open for business. It should be noted that during the period of the line's construction the London & North Western Railway (LNWR) was created in April 1846. In this picture a down Euston to Liverpool Lime Street restaurant car express, 'The Shamrock', is seen leaving Rugby in the evening sunshine behind 'Princess Coronation' Class Pacific No.46240 *City of Coventry* on 9th September 1961. This train connected at Liverpool with overnight sailings to Ireland, hence its name. In the winter 1959 timetable the journey time to Liverpool on Mondays to Fridays was exactly four hours northbound but in the opposite direction 4hrs 20min was allowed, possibly because there were more advertised stops. 'The Shamrock' was one of three named express services between London and Liverpool at that time, the others being 'The Red Rose' and 'The Merseyside Express'; the last mentioned train conveyed through carriages to and from Southport. *City of Coventry* was among the last batch of these locomotives withdrawn from service in September 1964 and at the time of writing one of its nameplates can be seen at Coventry station. *Neville Simms*

Inset: One of the nameplates carried by *City of Coventry*. This picture was taken at Rugby on 3rd February 1962. *Neville Simms*

Winter at Nettle Hill. Located north of Rugby between the former stations of Brinklow and Shilton, Nettle Hill is an appealing photographic spot where the West Coast Main Line (WCML) runs alongside the Oxford canal. In this picture Stanier Class 5MT No.44747 heads northwards in arctic conditions in charge of a very long goods train. This portrait was taken on 26th January 1963 during the 'Big Freeze' when Great Britain was gripped by bitterly cold weather for many weeks – note that the canal has frozen over and the intrepid photographer was therefore able to take a photograph not normally obtainable! No.44747 was one of a batch of these rather unattractive machines equipped with Caprotti valve gear. *Neville Simms*

Late summer at Nettle Hill. The bitter weather earlier in the year was probably a distant memory when this shot of 'Royal Scot' Class 7P No.46156 *The South Wales Borderer* heading north was taken on 20th September 1963. When this scene was recorded No.46156 had almost exactly a year remaining in service, being withdrawn in October 1964. Note that during the period since the previous picture was taken considerable progress had been made with electrification and the overhead wires are *in situ*. The intermediate stations between Rugby and Nuneaton were early closure casualties, both Brinklow and Shilton losing their passenger facilities from 16th September 1957 while Bulkington closed as early as 18th May 1931. *Neville Simms*

A southbound civil engineer's working, hauled by former LNWR 7F Class 0-8-0 No.49439, passes through Nuneaton Trent Valley station on a sunny 9th September 1961. There had been an engine shed at Nuneaton since the 1850s and the depot there was particularly busy; in 1939 it had as many as 80 locomotives allocated, almost half of which were LNWR 0-8-0s, the last of these engines being transferred away in 1962. Electric working started to Nuneaton in March 1964 but the shed lingered on until closure came on 6th June 1966. Sporadic steam workings continued for some time thereafter, one of the last being the visit of 8F Class No.48459 on an oil train from Ellesmere Port on 4th March 1967, three years after the wires had been energised! *Neville Simms*

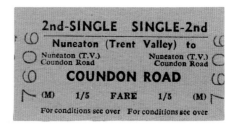

This remarkable piece of equipment probably came in with the *Rocket* – perhaps it could be described as an early example of 'Rocket Science'! This vintage, portable train indicator is thought to have dated from LNWR days but apparently was still in everyday use at Nuneaton station when this picture was taken on 22nd February 1964. Presumably it usually contained a variety of fingerboards but only two were visible on the day the shot was taken – perhaps the others had been 'claimed' by souvenir hunters. For the record the other board proclaimed 'Crewe, Warrington, Wigan, Preston and Blackpool'. *The late H W Robinson / Neville Simms collection*

Better late than never. A snowy scene at Ashby Junction, about a mile north-west of Nuneaton, showing the London-bound 'Ulster Express' approaching on 29th December 1962. The 'Ulster Express' ran between London and Heysham, where it connected with Belfast sailings, and on this particular day was running about two hours late with 'Black Five' No.45058 piloting 'Jubilee' No.45592 *Indore*. The train may have been held up at Heysham awaiting the arrival of the boat, of course, but it is more likely that it had been delayed by a diesel locomotive failure or simply lost time due to the bitterly cold weather that was causing havoc across Great Britain at that time. The passengers may have arrived in the Capital rather late but at least they would have been warm during the journey – some diesel-hauled trains were unheated due to their train heating boilers being out of action. On the right 8F Class 2-8-0 No.48349, hauling a goods train from the Shackerstone area, waits for the 'road' onto the main line.
Tommy Tomalin

A southbound parcels train, hauled by Stanier Class 5MT No.44761, is depicted just south of Lichfield Trent Valley station on 19th May 1964. Out-shopped from Crewe works in October 1947, No.44761 was destined to survive almost until the end of steam, not being withdrawn until April 1968. *Tony Sullivan*

Playing to the gallery. A Manchester to London express, headed by 'Royal Scot' Class 7P 4-6-0 No.46111 *Royal Fusilier*, rushes through Lichfield Trent Valley station on 2nd August 1959. The admiring audience includes a lady holding a young boy aloft, who is clearly a budding train spotter, and a lad wearing his school blazer and cap. No.46111 was one of fourteen 'Royal Scot' class locomotives based at Longsight, Manchester, shed at that time, mainly for use on London expresses. It is interesting to note that in 1959 the journey time from Manchester to Euston was more than 3 hours. *Tony Sullivan*

An up stopping train, with a respectably clean Stanier 'Jubilee' Class 4-6-0 No.45655 *Keith* in charge, pauses at Lichfield on 24th June 1958. The covered steps to the high level station can be seen immediately behind the engine while in the background the scene is dominated by the local maltings and, on the right, a water tank supported on a brick base. The high level platforms are today served by electric trains to and from Birmingham via Sutton Coldfield while, at the time of the photograph, irregular and infrequent trains also ran between Wolverhampton and Burton-on-Trent via Lichfield, a route which lost its passenger service from 18th January 1965. *Tony Sullivan*

The high and low level stations at Lichfield were connected by a spur line and in this shot Stanier Class 5MT No.44825 is depicted descending towards the main line tracks with a goods train on 22nd August 1964. Lichfield Trent Valley station's up platform is visible on the right and beyond it the bridge carrying the South Staffordshire line across the WCML. Strangely, between 18th January 1965 and 28th November 1988 no passenger trains operated between Lichfield Trent Valley high level and Lichfield City station, on the Sutton Coldfield route, that stretch of line being used solely by goods trains. *Tony Sullivan*

The starting signal is 'off' and the driver is looking out for the 'right away' from the guard. This further photograph taken at the north end of Lichfield Trent Valley station, shows the 3.35pm London to Manchester train awaiting departure behind 'Royal Scot' Class 7P 4-6-0 No.46106 *Gordon Highlander* on 24th June 1958. This particular engine was unique because it was the only member of its class fitted with distinctive, straight-sided smoke deflectors. Like No.46111, seen in a previous picture, *Gordon Highlander* was one of the substantial stud of these machines based at Longsight shed. Apart from one or two early diesel types, steam traction had a monopoly on the WCML at this time but this was broken within a year when the first diesel locomotives produced under the modernisation programme started to roll off the production lines. *Tony Sullivan*

A picture taken at Atherstone on 23rd May 1961 showing the 11.45am Liverpool Lime Street to Rugby train drawing to a halt with Stanier 'Jubilee' Class 6P/5F 4-6-0 No.45737 *Atlas* in charge. The station building, with its decorative roof tiles and multi-coloured brickwork, is a joy but, in the author's opinion, the rather functional platform canopy does little to enhance the station's otherwise attractive appearance. Clearly, there was little room for a signal box at Atherstone and its ingenious design, mounted between the tracks on steel girders with horizontal beams, takes up the minimum amount of space. The box's location gave the signalman a superb grandstand view of train movements and here the signalman on duty can be seen admiring the view from a window. One wonders, however, what it must have been like in the box if the windows were open when a slow moving goods train passed by with its locomotive belching smoke! *Hugh Ballantyne*

3rd-SINGLE   SINGLE-3rd

Atherstone to

Atherstone   Atherstone
Nuneaton (T.V.)   Nuneaton (T.V.)

NUNEATON (T.V.)

(M)   0/11   FARE   0/11   (M)

For conditions see over   For conditions see over

7640   7640

Stafford engine shed, officially known as the motive power depot, is the principal subject of this picture which was taken on 16th September 1961; note that the coaling plant's wagon hoist is in operation. The Grand Junction Railway stabled locomotives at Stafford from the opening of the line but a building was not provided until the 1850s, when a shed capable of holding 12 engines was constructed by the LNWR. In the 1860s Stafford was on the boundary of the LNWR's southern and northern divisions and it was decreed that a new, independent shed should be provided for the sole use of the southern division and many express passenger locomotives were subsequently based there. Stafford shed's importance faded, however, its allocation reduced and the crumbling, original shed building was demolished in the late 1930s. Despite the depot's diminished role the LMSR invested in a new, 60ft turntable and coaling plant during this period. The shed finally closed on 19th July 1965 and its remaining allocation was either withdrawn or transferred away. *Tommy Tomalin*

Various rival schemes were proposed in the early nineteenth century for a railway linking London and Birmingham; some of the promoters favoured a route via Oxford while others preferred one through Rugby and Coventry. The position was resolved in 1830 when the rival companies decided to merge and Robert Stephenson with his father were appointed joint engineers, a bill being deposited in Parliament on 20th February 1832. The idea of a railway line linking the two cities provoked a storm of protest from landowners who vehemently objected to the planned route. Stormy public meetings were arranged in places such as Berkhamsted and Watford and the matter was raised in the House of Lords where Lord Brownlow of Ashridge and others forcefully voiced their disapproval. The inevitable result was that the application for an Act of Parliament was rejected, but at least the promoters lived to fight another day. A second Bill received the Royal Assent on 6th May 1833 after alterations were made to the route in Hertfordshire and the compensation offered to landowners was considerably increased; construction began in November 1833 by which time Robert Stephenson was the sole engineer in charge. On 20th July 1837 the first section of the London & Birmingham Railway opened from Euston station to Boxmoor (Hemel Hempstead) while the first trains left Rugby for Birmingham (Curzon Street) on 9th April 1838. The line was not completely finished in time for the coronation of Queen Victoria on 28th June 1838 but, aware of the lucrative traffic this event would generate, the company advertised the first, limited services from 24th June 1838. The line was fully opened on 17th September 1838 and the journey time for the 112½ miles between London and Birmingham was 5½ hours. Two of the route's more notable engineering works, Beechwood tunnel and the Avon viaduct at Wolston, are located on the section between Rugby and Birmingham. A Blackpool to London train is seen accelerating away from Rugby at Hillmorton on 17th August 1963; motive power is provided by 'Royal Scot' Class 4-6-0 No.46125 *3rd Carabinier*. The steelwork is in place for the forthcoming electrification but no wires had appeared by the time of this photograph. By 1963 the once-common 'Royal Scot' Class locomotives were starting to become rare on West Coast Main Line express passenger duties due to the influx of diesels. In 1962 no fewer than 30 out of the original fleet of 71 locomotives were taken out of traffic with a further fifteen condemned in 1963, and by the end of 1964 a mere five survived. No.46125 was destined to last a further year after this shot was taken. *Neville Simms*

The best view in town? In times gone by it was essential that signalmen had an uninterrupted view of the line and those employed at the box just south of Rugby Midland station actually looked out onto two main lines, the WCML and the Great Central, which passed over the 'Premier Line' on the famous 'Birdcage' bridge, as it was universally known. In this shot a goods train, headed by Stanier 8F Class 2-8-0 No.48624, appears to be making good progress as it steams southwards on 25th March 1961. Note that the locomotive is running with a Fowler-type tender. The tracks veering off to the left led to Market Harborough, a cross country route that lost its passenger trains on 6th June 1966. *Charles Firminger*

L. M. & S. R.
FOR CONDITIONS SEE NOTICES
NOT VALID IN TRAINS   (M

PLATFORM TICKET
RUGBY(MIDLAND)
Issued Free
This ticket must be given up when leav-
ing Platform or at the time of booking

9107   9107

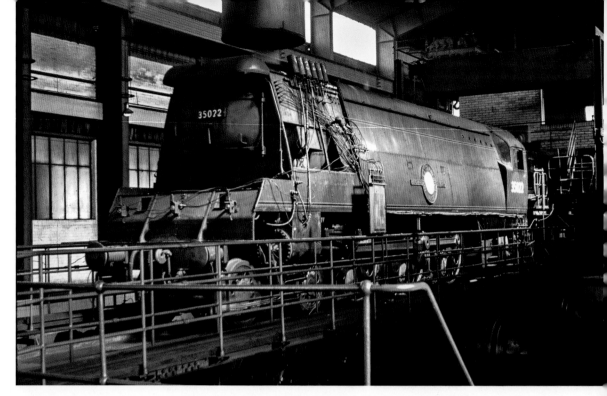

Sir Nigel Gresley stressed the desirability of establishing a national locomotive testing station during his Presidential address to the Institution of Locomotive Engineers in September 1927. Three years later a site was earmarked on the outskirts of Leeds but an appeal for funds was turned down by the government due to the severe economic recession prevailing at the time. The GWR already had a testing facility at Swindon while the SR was pressing ahead with electrification and saw this as its way forward. In 1937 the LMSR and LNER joined forces and decided to go ahead after evaluating testing plants at Vitry in France and Altoona in the United States. Construction at Rugby began in late 1938 and work was well advanced when brought abruptly to a halt when World War Two broke out in September 1939. Building resumed after the end of hostilities and the plant officially opened in October 1948. A total of 26 different locomotives were put through their paces at Rugby, the first being, appropriately, LNER A4 Class Pacific No.60007 *Sir Nigel Gresley* in October 1948. The 4-6-0 and 2-10-0 types accounted for most of the evaluation carried out at Rugby which was mainly concerned with testing various kinds of locomotive valve gear, chimneys and even mechanical stokers. In this picture Bulleid 'Merchant Navy' Class Pacific No.35022 *Holland-America Line* is seen undergoing testing on an unknown date in the early 1950s. It is recorded that this engine made three separate visits to Rugby to evaluate different types of blastpipe. One wonders whether the machine's coal consumption was measured! *J M Jarvis / Kidderminster Railway Museum*

A portrait of BR Standard 'Britannia' Class Pacific No.70025 *Western Star* taken at Rugby testing plant in November 1953. No.70025 was one of two 'Britannias' tested at Rugby, the other being No.70005 *John Milton* in 1951/52. In 1955 sister engine No.70026 *Polar Star,* which was powering an excursion from South Wales, was involved in a serious derailment near Didcot which resulted in eleven fatalities, and injuries were sustained by 157 passengers. During the subsequent inquiry it was suggested that the driver's forward vision had been impaired by the locomotive's handrails and, in an effort to improve visibility, six hand holds were cut into the smoke deflectors of some 'Britannias' allocated to the WR. *J M Jarvis / Kidderminster Railway Museum*

Three schoolboys, plus another apparently standing on the track, are captivated by the undoubtedly impressive sight of Stanier 'Princess Royal' Pacific No.46208 *Princess Helena Victoria* taking water at the south end of Rugby Midland station on 5th May 1962; it was working a train from Llandudno to London. In early 1961 the entire 'Princess Royal' Class was stored as 'surplus to requirements' but most re-entered traffic for the summer service, after which six were withdrawn and the rest returned to store. There was a motive power shortage in early 1962 and the six remaining engines again went back into service but only until the autumn when the survivors of this celebrated design were finally withdrawn. *Neville Simms*

Portrait of a faded star. In April 1935, to commemorate the 25 year reign of King George V, it was decided to name one of Stanier's three cylinder 4-6-0s *Silver Jubilee*. The locomotives were being built at that time and No.5642, which was the latest locomotive to be built, permanently exchanged numbers with No.5552. The 'new' No.5552 was painted in high gloss black enamel with chromium plated letters and numerals, dome cover and boiler bands. It was exhibited at Euston station on 2nd/3rd May 1935 and formed a prominent part of the LMSR's celebrations to mark that historic royal occasion. This shot of No.45552 was taken at Rugby shed on 13th July 1963; it seems to have been quite a nomadic engine and in the 1950s/60s was based at Carlisle (Kingmoor), Edge Hill and Crewe North sheds. *Neville Simms*

Sunlight and shadows. A portrait of Rugby Midland station, looking southwards, as it was on 16th September 1961. The maroon information signs dangling from the roof direct passengers to the cafeteria and bar and also indicate the office from where telegrams could be sent. Note the gas lighting and rather untidy state of the platform with a selection of barrows and other equipment lying around. The station seen here was actually the third to be built in the town, in 1885, and at one time the roofing was much more extensive than that seen here. The signal box is Rugby No.2 and the track to the right is the down through line while the platform road was able to accommodate two trains simultaneously due to the provision of the crossover. During the 1960s Rugby Midland suffered the loss of most of its secondary routes as a result of the cuts during the Beeching era. The ticket office at Rugby was originally located on the platform and not at street level but this situation was rectified in 2008 during extensive rebuilding as part of the upgrading of the WCML. *J J Smith / Bluebell Railway Museum*

Once maintained in spotless condition by Stewarts Lane shed for use on the prestigious 'Golden Arrow' boat train from London Victoria to Dover Marine, the glory days were over for BR Standard 'Britannia' Pacific No.70004 *William Shakespeare* when it was photographed passing Rugby on a London-bound goods train on 23rd May 1964. No.70004 was used on the Southern Region from the early 1950s until 1958 when, together with sister engine No.70014 *Iron Duke,* it was transferred to Trafford Park depot, Manchester, for use on London St. Pancras expresses over the demanding Peak route. Predictably, perhaps, the move coincided with a marked deterioration in the external condition of both locomotives which no longer received the special attention lavished upon them at Stewarts Lane. Note the slots or holes beneath the locomotive's nameplate which presumably enabled the side arrows to be affixed when working the 'Golden Arrow'. *Neville Simms*

The uniform rake of coaches in carmine and cream livery and lower quadrant signals immediately indicate that this photograph was taken many years ago and, indeed, it dates from 1952. Here, rebuilt 'Patriot' 7P Class 4-6-0 No.45535 *Sir Herbert Walker K.C.B.* is seen approaching Rugby Midland station in charge of a London-bound express. No.45535 was originally built at Derby and out-shopped in May 1933, but between 1946 and 1949 it was rebuilt, together with seventeen of its sister engines, with a larger taper boiler, double chimney and new cylinders. *J M Jarvis / Kidderminster Railway Museum*

This further vintage colour picture from the 1950s illustrates a completely different kind of train, in this case a slow moving, southbound goods train hauled by Hughes/Fowler 5MT Class 2-6-0 No.42891. A total of 245 of these locomotives was constructed between May 1926 and December 1932, the majority at Crewe but examples were also built at Horwich. Due to their high running plate and pitch of the cylinders, which gave them a rather ungainly appearance, these machines were universally known as 'Crabs'. They may not have been elegant, but the 'Crabs' were certainly very popular engines due to their free steaming and sure-footed characteristics which were a boon to enginemen working heavy goods trains in wet conditions. Note the wooden bodied wagons forming part of the train and also, on the right, a number of partially hidden vans that appear to bear the initials of the LMSR. *J M Jarvis / Kidderminster Railway Museum*

A panoramic view of the substantial layout at the north end of Rugby station with nicely cleaned Stanier-designed Class 4MT 2-6-4T No.42562 leaving in charge of the 4.44pm Rugby (Midland) to Nuneaton (Trent Valley) local train on 9th September 1961. The signal box in the centre of the picture is Rugby No.5. The massive layout seen here has been very much reduced but Rugby still has one notable railway landmark, the flyover north of the station which was brought into regular use on 17th September 1962, being part of the improvements associated with the WCML electrification. Full electric working between Rugby and Crewe commenced on 4th January 1965. *Neville Simms*

Holbrook Park water troughs were located about two miles west of Rugby and in this photograph the fireman of 'Royal Scot' Class 7P No.46147 *The Northamptonshire Regiment* has lowered the scoop to replenish the tender's water supply – woe betide anybody foolish enough to lean out of the window! No.46147 was powering the 8.45am Euston to Wolverhampton train via Northampton on the rather dismal summer Saturday of 30th June 1962. *Neville Simms*

Coventry station's No.1 signal box is a prominent feature of this illustration which shows the junction of the Rugby and Leamington Spa lines at the east end of the station on 10th May 1961. Coventry locomotive shed is partially concealed by the signal box, but one or two engines can just be discerned on the extreme right of the shot. This shed dated from 1866 and was erected in the fork of the Rugby and Leamington lines; it was accessed from the latter. The shed probably reached the peak of its importance in the 1930s when about twenty locomotives were based there but any major attention required was undertaken at Rugby, the parent depot. BR undertook repairs to the roof in the 1950s but this expenditure unfortunately coincided with a substantial decline in local trip work and the shed closed on 17th November 1958. Despite its official closure the shed took on a new lease of life as a locomotive storage depot, a role that continued for at least six years; in late 1963 the occupants were five 'Jubilee' Class 4-6-0s. *The late H W Robinson / Neville Simms collection*

Coventry station during rebuilding. A train bound for Birmingham, headed by Stanier Class 5MT No.45038 waits at the west end of Coventry station in October 1959. When reconstruction began in 1959 the station and inadequate track layout then *in situ* dated back to the 1880s and radical, extensive improvement was required in preparation for electrification. During the Second World War much of Coventry city centre was destroyed by German air attacks but, remarkably, the station buildings escaped without damage. Temporary wooden buildings were erected to accommodate the administrative offices during reconstruction and following the demolition of the parcels bridge a shuttle service had to be operated between the platforms with a locomotive and parcels van. Warwick Road overbridge spanned two tracks only and restricted expansion, so this was replaced by a wide-span concrete bridge which enabled Platform No.1 to be lengthened by a considerable distance. The junctions to Leamington Spa and Nuneaton were both re-sited as far away from the station as physical limitations would permit. During the modernisation works on the WCML and consequent reduction in train services an enhanced frequency was provided between Birmingham and London Paddington to compensate. This did not benefit Coventry, however, and the drastic pruning of through London trains did little to endear BR to Coventry's Chamber of Commerce or the city's business circles. BR responded to criticism by providing additional morning and evening trains which, in one case, connected at Leamington Spa to and from Paddington while a further extra working was the 9.10am to Euston consisting of two carriages which were attached to the 6.45am Crewe to Euston at Rugby! The corresponding return service was the 6.15pm Euston to Crewe which conveyed a two-coach portion for Coventry. Regular weekend diversions, which sometimes caused the complete closure of the station, added to travellers' woes and sometimes they must have wondered if it was all worthwhile. *R C Riley*

The new Coventry station was officially opened on 1st May 1962 and while it may not have won many plaudits for architectural brilliance at least it was bright and functional; most of all, perhaps, it had much greater operational flexibility than the dilapidated premises it replaced. On 25th May the new Coventry cathedral was consecrated, an event which had almost as much impact on BR operations as the station opening. May 1962 was certainly a momentous month for the city! The new cathedral attracted trainloads of visitors from all over Great Britain and on 22nd September seven trains, from places as far apart as Blackpool and Brighton, converged on Coventry so it was just as well the station had four platforms by this date. This traffic continued for some time and in this shot, taken looking down on the new station, 'Patriot' Class 7P 4-6-0 No.45545 *Planet* almost looks out of place amid the new surroundings as

it awaits departure with a return excursion to Carlisle on 23rd October 1963. In the early 1960s some of the trains that called at Coventry were still steam hauled and the end of March 1963 reportedly saw a resurgence in the use of Stanier Pacifics on Euston trains which, while a joy for steam fans, must have dented the modern image that BR were striving to portray at that time. Locomotives of this class could still be seen sporadically on London trains a year later, presumably a result of the non-availability of English Electric Type 4 diesels (later Class 40). The annual Coventry holiday exodus, which in 1964 started on 11th July, provided a feast of steam traction for the enthusiast and of 30 specials provided only one was worked by diesel traction. Appropriately, No.46240 *City of Coventry* was provided to work the 5.00am to Eastbourne, presumably as far as Willesden. Steam could still be seen very occasionally at Coventry as late as February 1967. *Neville Simms*

A return excursion from Newcastle upon Tyne, run in connection with the opening of the new cathedral, awaits departure on 9th April 1963; motive power is Gresley V2 Class 2-6-2 No.60963 of York shed. A few days later B1 Class 4-6-0 No.61018 *Gnu* visited Coventry with a similar train from Sunderland. *Neville Simms*

Berkswell station, seen here in this shot taken on 12th September 1964, was known as 'Dockers Lane' until 1853 and a further change of name occurred from 1st February 1928 when the suffix 'Balsall Common' was adopted but the name subsequently reverted to 'Berkswell' in about 1960. A level crossing was situated immediately behind the photographer together with an underpass for pedestrians, a most unusual feature. Beyond the crossing was a small goods yard and signalbox, both being situated on the down side; the latter was taken out of use on 3rd July 1966. There is also a stationmaster's house on that side of the line and this is the only substantial building to have survived rationalisation. Berkswell was formerly a junction for Kenilworth but this line lost its passenger service on 18th January 1965. *Neville Simms*

Passengers using Berkswell station for the first time may have been surprised to find that the premises still depended on oil lamps for lighting after dark, so they would have to watch their step on a wet night. This fine specimen, which displays the old name of the station, was photographed on the same day as the previous picture. One wonders whether it survived modernisation and where it is now! *Neville Simms*

The former LNWR side of Birmingham New Street station was rather cramped which made it rather difficult to photograph trains, but here is a picture of Stanier 'Princess Coronation' Class Pacific No.46241 *City of Edinburgh* waiting to depart from Platform Three at the head of a train to Euston some time in 1962. It is likely that this train was not rostered for steam haulage and No.46241 was a last-minute substitute for a defective diesel locomotive. Note the coal pusher apparatus on the rear bulkhead of the tender. The start for eastbound trains could not have been easier, there was an initial falling gradient of 1 in 77 through New Street South tunnel, and favourable gradients continued as far as Hampton-in-Arden. What more could a hard working fireman ask for? *G J Jones / Kidderminster Railway Museum*

A distinguished visitor to New Street station on 20th May 1961 was the unique BR Standard Pacific No.71000 *Duke of Gloucester* which worked in on a train from Glasgow, though the photographer points out that it probably only powered it from Crewe. No.71000 was allocated to Crewe (North) shed at the time of the photograph. *Duke of Gloucester* was uncharacteristically clean for a locomotive allocated to Crewe North shed, which was not noted for keeping its stud in sparkling condition. Its pristine state in this picture almost certainly resulted from its appearance at an exhibition celebrating the golden jubilee of the Institution of Locomotive Engineers held at Marylebone a few days previously. Authorised as a replacement for 'Princess Royal' Pacific No.46202 *Princess Anne* which was damaged beyond repair in the Harrow accident of 8th October 1952, *Duke of Gloucester* entered service in May 1954 and was intended to be the prototype of a new BR Standard design. It is a three cylinder locomotive and is fitted with Caprotti valve gear and could be described as the ultimate in British steam locomotive design, but it proved disappointing in service and the BR modernisation plan of 1955 scuppered any thought of further examples being constructed. In view of its historical importance as the last express passenger engine built for use in Great Britain, a set of its cylinders and motion was removed upon withdrawal in November 1962 for public display and the rest was sold for scrap. Rescued from Barry in 1974, No.71000 underwent a painstaking restoration to main line condition during which it was discovered that the machine had not been built to the correct specification and this may have accounted for its lack-lustre performance in traffic. *Neville Simms*

A picture taken at Birmingham New Street in the summer of 1955 showing BR Standard 'Britannia' Pacific No.70044 awaiting departure with an unidentified passenger train. The locomotive was running experimentally with air brake equipment and without smoke deflectors; the ugly air pumps and cylinders positioned on the front of the smokebox hardly enhance the engine's appearance. Sister locomotive No.70043 was similarly equipped at the time and both locomotives were subsequently converted to conventional operation, later becoming *Earl Haig* and *Lord Kitchener* respectively. The unattractive, bare steel girders that supported the platform canopies on this side of the station gave the platforms a somewhat claustrophobic feel. *Mike Esau*

BIRMINGHAM (NEW STREET) TO WOLVERHAMPTON (HIGH LEVEL)

The Birmingham Wolverhampton & Stour Valley Railway obtained an Act in August 1846 to construct a line from a site in New Street, Birmingham, to Wolverhampton via Tipton. A branch from Smethwick to Stourbridge was also envisaged but this was abandoned before the Act was passed but, even so, the route is still known, rather misleadingly, as the 'Stour Valley Line'. Construction of the railway line, which was divided into three sections, started in 1847 from the southern end with an 845 yards-long tunnel immediately north of (what later became) New Street station; Robert Stephenson and William Baker were the engineers. Construction appears to have gone relatively smoothly and the first goods trains ran on 1st February 1852 and passenger from 1st July; the northern terminus was Wolverhampton Queen Street Station, known as High Level from 1st June 1885. The Shrewsbury & Birmingham Railway (SBR) had been given running powers over the line and a bitter feud between them and the LNWR (which had absorbed the local Stour Valley company) resulted in a court battle in which the SBR was victorious. On 1st May 1853 the LNWR introduced a half-hourly passenger service which effectively denied the SBR access but, from 4th February 1854, the SBR at last started to run through to New Street, after three years of bitter disputes. This arrangement proved short-lived, however, because from 13th November it switched to the newly opened Low Level station and ran instead to Snow Hill via Wednesbury. In this picture 'Royal Scot' Class 4-6-0 No.46134 *The Cheshire Regiment* is seen climbing past Monument Lane shed (out of the picture on the right) with a down express in the summer of 1955. *Mike Esau*

The first shed at Monument Lane opened in the 1850s but was hopelessly over-crowded and new premises were built in 1884. Despite the restricted nature of the site six roads were laid and a 42ft turntable installed; there was accommodation for around 30 locomotives. The shed's allocation continued to grow, however, and by 1925 it had risen to 45 engines and the shed was extremely crowded. The LMSR decided that another total rebuild was the only solution and in the early 1930s the second shed was demolished, a new shed built, and new coal and ash plants installed. This work was completed in 1934 and the premises also benefited from a 60ft turntable that had been installed some years earlier. After nationalisation steam declined at Monument Lane and the shed lost the last of its steam allocation at the start of the summer timetable in 1961, but visiting engines continued to be serviced until January 1962. Its last function was as a signing-on point for diesel train crews and it remained officially as a diesel depot as late as 1965; needless to say the buildings were later demolished. In this photograph, dating from the mid-1950s, the most prominent locomotive is Johnson 2F Class 0-6-0 No.58135, a Dubs & Co. product dating from 1875, while BR Standard 'Britannia' Pacific No.70042 *Lord Roberts* was from an altogether different age, having entered traffic in 1953. On the right a diesel shunting locomotive is just visible lurking in the depths of the shed. *Mike Esau*

BIRMINGHAM (NEW STREET) TO WOLVERHAMPTON (HIGH LEVEL)

Bearing in mind Wolverhampton's undoubted status as an important railway centre, on the basis of the photographs submitted for publication in this book, relatively few pictures seem to have been taken there. The author was pleased, therefore, when this shot was submitted showing Stanier 'Jubilee' Class 6P5F 4-6-0 No.45734 *Meteor,* in respectably clean condition, simmering prior to departure from the High Level station with a train to London Euston on 19th October 1959. Journey times between Wolverhampton/Birmingham and London at that time were inflated by modernisation works preparatory to electrification and, for example, in the winter 1959 timetable the 6.40am from Wolverhampton, one of the very few through trains, was not due into Euston until 10.13am. The LMR's winter 1959 timetable, which commenced on 2nd November, announced that the entire Wolverhampton to London service was being withdrawn from that date and passengers were advised to use the Western Region route. *R C Riley*

BIRMINGHAM (NEW STREET) TO WOLVERHAMPTON (HIGH LEVEL)

The London & Birmingham Railway was one of the first companies to show interest in serving Leamington Spa, surveying their proposed line from Coventry as early as 1836, but their ideas met with hostility from the local populace and were postponed for some years. The line was eventually opened on 9th December 1844 but only as far as Milverton; an extension to Leamington was authorised in 1846. In October 1852 the Birmingham & Oxford Railway opened through Leamington Spa and in 1864 a connection was built to link the Coventry and Oxford routes. This is the delightfully ornate interior of Kenilworth station's booking office, where the intricate wooden panelling would not be out of place at a stately home. Note the pictorial posters, advertising the virtues of Hertfordshire and Buxton, gas lighting and rack for handbills that looks rather out of place in such relatively palatial surroundings. The original specification clearly included two booking office windows – perhaps the architect was an eternal optimist! This picture was taken on 6th April 1963. *Tommy Tomalin*

The old LMSR-style 'hawkseye' nameboard immediately identifies the location of this photograph, Leamington Spa Avenue station, which was adjacent to the former GWR premises. This picture was taken looking eastwards, also on 6th April 1963. In addition to trains from Coventry, this station was also the terminating point for former LNWR branch services from Rugby and Weedon, but these were lightly used and withdrawn in 1959 and 1958 respectively. The summer 1961 timetable reveals that a roughly hourly service operated from Nuneaton to Leamington Spa via Coventry, but this was also considered to be unremunerative and closed to passengers on 18th January 1965. The track remained *in situ,* however, for goods traffic and the connection between the former LNWR and GWR lines was altered in 1966, being moved from the east end of Leamington Spa General Station to the west end, this coming into use from 15th May 1966. The line between Coventry and Leamington Spa was reopened for passengers in 1977 and passenger traffic has also been reinstated between Coventry and Nuneaton. *Neville Simms*

A stranger at Leamington. Four enthusiasts on the down platform and four railwaymen standing on the track appear to be transfixed as Bulleid 'Battle of Britain' Class Pacific No.34087 *145 Squadron* takes the Coventry line at Leamington Spa with the 8.00am Bournemouth to Coventry football special on 3rd November 1962. Their interest is probably explained by the fact that this was a rare manoeuvre for a passenger train. The connection at this end of Leamington Spa General station was, as previously mentioned, later moved to the other end of the layout. *J J Smith / Bluebell Railway Museum*

Situated in the fork of the Banbury and Rugby lines south of the station there had been an engine shed at Leamington Spa since 1852 but this was burnt down in 1902. A new four-road shed was erected as a replacement and this opened in 1906; it was the prototype of Churchward's straight shed design. Leamington shed's principal function was to provide motive power for Birmingham suburban services and passenger tank engines usually comprised most of its allocation of about 25 locomotives. The introduction of diesel units on those services in the 1950s certainly heralded a decline in the depot's work and its allocation was reportedly down to seventeen locomotives by October 1959. Closure came in June 1965 and the site is now occupied by industrial units. In this portrait of the shed, taken on 16th April 1963, it seems to be reasonably busy and 'Hall' Class 4-6-0 No.6926 *Holkham Hall* was a guest. Note the turntable on the far left of the picture. *Neville Simms*

Those were the days when restaurant car expresses linked Paddington and Birmingham (Snow Hill)/Birkenhead and vice versa and passengers from intermediate stations such as Leamington Spa were able to have lunch or dinner during the journey to London. Many trains were rostered for the mighty GWR 'King' Class locomotives, and in this vintage photograph taken at the north end of Leamington station on 11th December 1954, No.6006 *King George I*, pauses with a Wolverhampton-bound train. This machine was one of six examples of this class based at Stafford Road shed, Wolverhampton, at that time specifically for use on these services. The crack train on this route was 'The Inter-City' and there was even a sleeping car service between Paddington and Birkenhead (Woodside) until the route was downgraded by BR in March 1967. *R C Riley*

LEAMINGTON SPA TO BIRMINGHAM (SNOW HILL)

Oh dear, whatever happened to that much vaunted Great Western pride? Here, 'Castle' Class 4-6-0 No.7012 *Barry Castle*, in disgraceful external condition, enters Leamington Spa station with an inter-regional train from Wolverhampton to Ramsgate on 28th September 1963. Note the signal box, partially visible immediately to the right of the locomotive, which is on the former LNWR line to Coventry. The line between Leamington Spa and Adderley Street (near Bordesley station) was originally part of the Birmingham & Oxford Railway (BOR) that received the Royal Assent on 3rd August 1846. This line's southern limit was at Knightcote, two miles north of Fenny Compton, where it made an end-on connection with the projected Oxford & Rugby Railway. A short section of earthworks beyond Knightcote was constructed before the latter line was abandoned. The BOR, which was a mixed gauge, double track route was absorbed by the GWR on 31st August 1848, the section through Leamington Spa coming into use on 1st October 1852. The final 1¼ miles from Adderley Street to Livery Street station were built by the Birmingham Extension Railway and there a connection was made with the Birmingham Wolverhampton & Dudley Railway; in February 1858 Livery Street station was renamed Snow Hill. At that time Snow Hill station was a temporary affair with wooden structures but at least they must have been reasonably sound because the station roof was later removed to Didcot where it gave further service as part of a carriage shed. Broad gauge trains ceased to run between Oxford and Wolverhampton after 1st April 1869. The line immediately south of Snow Hill station passed through a deep cutting in the city centre before threading a tunnel and in 1874 the cutting was roofed over to provide space for shops; a shopping arcade was erected at that location in 1876. GWR journey times to London compared unfavourably with the rival LNWR and in an effort to speed up services slip coaches were introduced and water troughs laid to enable locomotives to take on further supplies without the need to stop. *Neville Simms*

Great Western pride is well in evidence in this photograph, however, which shows immaculate 'Castle' Class 4-6-0 No.5010 *Restormel Castle* departing from Leamington Spa General on 19th April 1957. The locomotive's copper capped chimney and safety valve bonnet have clearly been burnished to perfection and the rest of the engine looks to be in pristine condition in true GWR style. Regrettably, *Restormel Castle* became an early casualty, being withdrawn in October 1959, one of the first locomotives of its class to suffer this fate. The suffix 'General' was used between 1950 and 1968 and the former GWR station should not be confused with the adjacent, former LMSR Leamington Spa Avenue station which was closed from 18th January 1965. *R C Riley*

It is Christmas Eve 1962 and 5101 Class 2-6-2T No.4125 has been assigned to the Hatton banking duty; it is seen simmering in the bay at Warwick awaiting its next call to duty. The damp platform surface indicates there has just been a shower but the sun has burst through, no doubt pleasing the photographer. This shot provides a good view of the signal box and the signalman's preferred mode of conveyance! *Tommy Tomalin*

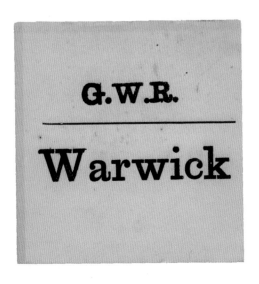

Northbound trains have favourable gradients all of the way from Fenny Compton to a spot just north of Leamington Spa where they encounter the start of the climb to Hatton station; gradients of around 1 in 108 apply for six miles to the summit. In this shot 'Castle' Class 4-6-0 No.5063 *Earl Baldwin* is depicted storming up the incline at the head of twelve coaches without a hint of leaking steam at the front end. One can only imagine the rousing exhaust noise as the locomotive, apparently working flat out, passed the photographer's viewpoint – absolutely brilliant! *Neville Simms*

Perfection on Hatton bank. The fireman of BR Standard Class 9F 2-10-0 No.92247 appears to be following the BR Fireman's Manual perfectly because there is not a trace of black smoke from the 9F's chimney and the escaping steam from the safety valves indicates there was plenty of steam available. Well done! No.92247 was working (what appears to be) a heavy train of iron ore wagons on 29th March 1965. It is sad to reflect that this locomotive had only been in service for 6¼ years at the time of this photograph and was, therefore, a relatively new engine but it was nonetheless taken out of traffic in December 1966 – what a waste! *Martin Smith*

One of the most memorable days for railway enthusiasts in the West Midlands was 27th April 1963 when Southampton played Manchester United in an FA Cup semi-final at Villa Park, Birmingham. No fewer than fifteen special trains ran from Southampton while six conveyed supporters from Manchester. Ten of the specials from Southampton ran via Basingstoke and Oxford, nine of which were powered by Bulleid Pacifics throughout, the tenth being worked by 'Modified Hall' No.7919 *Runter Hall* from Reading. Three others travelled via Oxford and Worcester to Birmingham Snow Hill and were piloted up the bank to Rowley Regis by 8F Class 2-8-0s from Stourbridge shed, the combination of a Bulleid Pacific piloted by an 8F being most unusual. A special from Brockenhurst was routed via the Somerset & Dorset line and then via Gloucester to New Street while the final train, from Eastleigh, went via Southampton, Salisbury, Westbury and Bristol; both of the last-mentioned were hauled by 'Jubilees' from either Bristol or Bath. What a day it must have been for enthusiasts in the Birmingham area! Here Bulleid Pacific No.34040 *Crewkerne* is depicted passing a spectator on Hatton bank. *Neville Simms*

Stanier Class 5MT No.44872 makes an energetic assault on Hatton bank with a Festiniog Railway Society special train on 23rd April 1966. The locomotive appears to have undergone some rather haphazard cleaning: the boiler is shining a little but the tender is covered with grime. Perhaps No.44872 was a substitute for another locomotive that failed at the last minute. *Derek Huntriss*

The 12.10pm Paddington to Birmingham train, headed by 'King' Class 4-6-0 No.6005 *King George II*, was photographed ascending Hatton bank on 22nd October 1962. Services on the Paddington-Birmingham-Birkenhead route had been largely dieselised by this date using 'Western' class diesel hydraulic locomotives and deep inroads had been made into the ranks of the 'King' class engines. A mere five members were still active by this time and the photographer no doubt considered himself very lucky to obtain this shot of a 'King' during their final few weeks of operation. Bearing in mind it was facing oblivion, No.6005 is in very presentable external condition. *Martin Smith*

G. W. R.

Hatton

Mechanical signalling has been in use since the early days of railways but is becoming increasingly harder to find as technology advances, thus enabling large areas to be controlled from a single signalling centre: even the much vaunted power boxes of the 1960s are being made redundant. The maintenance of mechanical equipment is very costly with miles of point rodding and signal wires as exemplified here in this picture taken at the west end of Hatton station; the signal arms on the left were for the Stratford-upon-Avon branch while the others signalled the Birmingham route. Amazingly, at one time there were no fewer than four signal boxes at Hatton but this was reduced to three in 1936. Mechanical signalling became a thing of the past at Hatton when the remaining boxes were closed in September 1969. This picture was taken on 20th June 1964. *Neville Simms*

Left: A loss of dignity? The introduction of English Electric Type 4 locomotives on the WCML spelled doom for large numbers of 'Royal Scot' Class 4-6-0s and those locomotives that survived were relegated to mundane goods duties as seen here. At least No.46122 *Royal Ulster Rifleman* is still in reasonably clean condition as it climbs Hatton bank on an unknown date in the early 1960s. No.46122 survived to become one of the last representatives of its class in traffic, not being withdrawn until October 1964, by which time 'Royal Scots' were very thin on the ground. *John Tarrant/ Kidderminster Railway Museum*

The final full year of operation of 'Castle' Class locomotives in the Birmingham area was 1964 and when this picture of 'Castle' Class 4-6-0 No.5056 *Earl of Powis* picking up water from Lapworth troughs was taken on 22nd August 1964 few regular passenger duties remained for the class. Most of the 'Castle' turns were on inter-regional holiday trains such as the Manchester Piccadilly to Bournemouth working depicted in this shot; No.5056 had presumably taken over at either Wolverhampton Low Level or Birmingham Snow Hill. Other summer extras that were steam-hauled from Snow Hill at this time included the 9.45am to Margate, 10.05am to Torquay and 10.42am to Margate; on 8th August 1964 the last mentioned was powered by 'Castle' No.7024 *Powis Castle*. The 5.45pm FO from Snow Hill to Paddington was still rostered for a 'Castle' as late as 30th October when No.7029 *Clun Castle* appeared, but everything else on that route was normally diesel-worked. *Neville Simms*

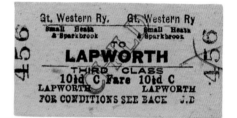

This view looking northwards from Lapworth station is thought to have been taken in the late 1950s. Note the flower beds and busy goods yard on the right of the picture; the yard was closed in November 1963. Originally known as Kingswood, the station opened in 1854 and underwent a change of identity on 1st May 1902 and has been known as Lapworth ever since. Originally Lapworth was located on a double track line but in the early 1930s the GWR quadrupled the route from Olton, eight miles to the north, to increase capacity and many new bridges were constructed to accommodate the extra tracks. That section reverted to double track only in 1968. In times gone by Lapworth was the junction for Henley-in-Arden but the passenger service was very short-lived, operating only from 1894 to 1915 by which time the more direct line from Tyseley was available. *Stuart Ackley collection*

The 1960s was a period of retrenchment on the railways and BR decided that the luxury of four tracks as far as Lapworth could no longer be justified in the harsh financial climate they faced at that time. The additional tracks the GWR had laid only 35 years earlier were dispensed with and in this picture, taken at Solihull on 29th September 1968, lifting is already in progress. The locomotive on the right is unmistakable; yes, it is preserved Gresley Pacific No.4472 *Flying Scotsman* which was passing through on a rail tour. *Tony Sullivan*

Equally unmistakable, but for altogether different reasons, is WD Class 2-8-0 No.90565 which is seen ambling along with a lengthy train of empty coal wagons between Olton and Solihull on 26th April 1962. The humble WDs were amongst the unsung workhorses of the BR steam era and worked at various times on all BR regions, often hauling mineral trains of the type seen here. A total of 934 of these war-time 'Austerity' machines was built by the North British Locomotive Co. and Vulcan Foundry, this particular example being out-shopped by the latter in September 1943. It was originally No.77102 and entered BR stock in December 1948; it was taken out of service in October 1962. *Tony Sullivan*

The name of the adjacent warehouse is proudly displayed in the stonework and immediately identifies the location of this photograph. Birmingham Moor Street station was opened to passenger traffic on 1st July 1909 and the adjacent goods shed on 7th January 1914. The passenger station was built to cater for increasing suburban traffic from the city's southern suburbs and relieve pressure on Snow Hill. The station originally had four terminal platforms; however there was a scarcity of land and little room was available so two traversers were installed at the buffer stop ends of the platforms to save space. Traversers were sometimes used in railway works but their use in a passenger station in place of run-round loops was exceedingly rare; they were taken out of use in December 1967. This picture, taken on 17th July 1963, shows the compact nature of the station and its attractive architecture which is totally dwarfed by neighbouring buildings. After years of neglect the terminal buildings at Moor Street were beautifully restored to GWR style by Chiltern Railways in association with local organisations and the bay platforms became fully operational again in 2010. *Lens of Sutton Association*

The 5.10pm to Leamington Spa, with beautifully clean 8100 Class 2-6-2T No.8109 in charge, awaits departure from Snow Hill station on 16th April 1963. The glass screens on the right of the picture no doubt prevented annoying draughts besides being a decorative feature. Despite the widespread use of diesel units on suburban services radiating from Snow Hill from the late 1950s some rush hour workings remained steam hauled into the mid-1960s. During the summer of 1964 the 5.28pm to Knowle & Dorridge was reportedly the preserve of restored tank engine No.4555 while the 5.52pm to Evesham via the North Warwickshire Line was booked for a 'Hall' class locomotive from Tyseley. The last booked main line steam workings into Snow Hill occurred on 4th September 1965 when two summer Saturday holiday trains from Devon to Wolverhampton produced 'Britannia' Pacifics. The *very* last steam powered train on the route, however, was powered by 'Castle' Class 4-6-0 No.7029 *Clun Castle* which hauled the 12.30pm Penzance to Wolverhampton forward from Bristol, thus providing a fitting end to the steam-hauled summer holiday trains between Birmingham and the South-West. This locomotive was used following a suggestion by the Cheltenham branch of the Railway Correspondence & Travel Society. *Neville Simms*

BRITISH TRANSPORT COMMISSION
BRITISH RAILWAYS   B.R. 21716/75

BIRMINGHAM
SNOW HILL

The routes from Oxford and Wolverhampton to Birmingham, both of which were promoted in the 1840s by independent companies, made an end-on junction in the centre of the city where a new station was proposed. Both of the independent companies had been absorbed into the GWR before the station (known as Snow Hill from February 1858) opened on 1st October 1852. This wooden structure proved to be totally inadequate and was replaced in 1871 by larger premises while, during the intervening period, the Great Western Hotel was opened in 1863 above the tracks at the south end of the station. This impressive building, which boasted 126 rooms, was one of the finest Victorian buildings in the city. Despite the enlargement Snow Hill station could not cope with increasing traffic and in November 1902 the sum of £341,693 was authorised for the rebuilding of the station, work beginning in earnest in September 1906. Some of the pressure on Snow Hill was eased when Moor Street station was opened in July 1909 to handle suburban traffic from the southern suburbs. The 'new' Snow Hill, opened in 1912, was apparently ranked No.3 in the GWR's table of best stations and had three times the platform length of the old premises. The rebuilt station consisted of two very spacious island platforms, separated by two goods lines, with bays at the north end. Three of the four principal through platforms were almost 1,200ft in length and could accommodate two trains simultaneously; they had intermediate scissors crossovers that gave considerable operational flexibility and enabled a train at the bottom of a platform to overtake one standing in front. An especially pleasant aspect of the station's design was the overall roof, the centre portion of which was open to the sky; this enabled smoke to escape whilst admitting fresh air and sunlight. Another development was the closure of the GWR hotel, which had not proved popular due to its very close proximity to the railway tracks, and in 1909 it was closed and converted to railway offices with a public restaurant on the ground floor. During the same year the station was equipped with an advanced electrically operated semaphore signalling system worked from two boxes, one at each end of the station. The north box stood in an elevated position on braced steel stanchions, its peculiar design being dictated by the extremely limited amount of space available. The booking office boasted two Regina automatic ticket printing machines, the first to be installed in Great Britain, and these required only blank cards to be stocked; a duplicate was automatically printed for accounting purposes. In 1937 Snow Hill became one of the first stations on the GWR to be equipped with a public address system. In more recent years, despite the planned electrification of the West Coast Main Line, which included much of the network in the Birmingham area, the Western Region invested in modern colour light signalling which was controlled from a new building on the down platform; this was brought into use on 11th September 1960. In 1961 BR announced plans to rebuild the station while a passenger census in 1964 revealed that, in spite of some reductions of services, Snow Hill still handled a third of all passenger traffic from central Birmingham. The electrification of the line from Euston in March 1967 meant that Snow Hill was doomed as a main line station, but two local services defiantly continued despite the LMR's best efforts to close them. On 5th May 1969 it suffered the ultimate indignity when it became famous as the largest unstaffed halt in Great Britain and in 1978 BR demolished the derelict premises after cracks appeared in the brickwork. Later the realisation dawned that, even in a city dominated by the motor car, building new roads very often exacerbated rather than relieved traffic problems and Snow Hill was destined to be born again. The deserted platforms and shuttered newspaper kiosk seen in this picture tell their own story; this shot was taken on 5th July 1967, four months after the station had been stripped of its main line status. The eerie silence, which had replaced the station's former hustle and bustle, was broken only by the occasional local train – how sad. *Roy Denison*

The imposing, massive facade of Snow Hill station is depicted in this portrait taken on 5th July 1967. GWR pride was still very evident in the 1960s when people were interviewed by a local newspaper. Many considered Snow Hill, with its long, wide platforms, to be a better station than New Street and had memories of steam-hauled goods trains roaring through on the centre roads. Two local services, to Wolverhampton Low Level and Langley Green, sometimes formed of a single car, clung on until withdrawn from 6th March 1972 when the local passenger transport executive withdrew financial support and, regrettably, demolition followed. A new, four platform station was opened on 5th October 1987 but by that time one of Great Britain's finest main line stations was just a fading memory. *Roy Denison*

The Birmingham Wolverhampton & Dudley Railway (BWDR) was promoted at a time when the competing Shrewsbury & Birmingham Railway (SBR) was also seeking powers to link Wolverhampton with Birmingham. The former envisaged a connection with the Birmingham Extension Railway at Livery Street station (later Snow Hill) while the latter was focused on New Street. The proposers of the BWDR took their case to a select committee of the House of Commons presenting their line as a purely local venture that wished to serve as many works and collieries in the area as practicable and, moreover, unlike the rival SBR, its construction would cause very little destruction of property in the centre of Birmingham compared to the SBR. The BWDR's greatest virtue, however, was stated to be its locally controlled, totally independent status which would enable it to focus on the needs of the local population free of interference from the domineering London & Birmingham Railway (LBR) at Euston Square. The committee heard representations from a variety of witnesses including some, inevitably, who were hardly impartial and had links to the BWDR. The idea of an independent route appealed to John Barker, a Wolverhampton iron master, while Lord Hatherton was antagonistic towards the SBR because it would destroy some of his land and create a huge monopoly if it later merged with the LBR. A local MP also spoke of his fear of a monopoly situation and said that only competition would compel the LBR to act in the interests of the travelling public. The BWDR was authorised on 3rd August 1846 and formal opening was proposed for 1st September 1854, but this had to be deferred when a bridge collapsed and the line eventually opened on 14th November after a programme of bridge strengthening had been completed. The BWDR was mixed gauge initially but broad gauge trains were withdrawn from 1st November 1864. Main line stations where goods trains pass through on the middle roads always have a particular appeal, some of the best examples being Manchester Victoria in times past, Eastleigh and Doncaster. In this photograph 'Hall' Class No.4923 *Evenley Hall* is seen threading the complex pointwork to the north of Birmingham Snow Hill station with a train of hopper wagons in tow on 16th April 1963. Some of the people on the opposite platform are clutching notebooks and look suspiciously like train spotters – one wonders if they 'copped' No.4923. It may well have been a 'cop' for visiting spotters but those locally based are likely to have been disappointed because at the time *Evenley Hall* was allocated to Oxley shed just up the road at Wolverhampton. *Neville Simms*

An FA Cup match at Villa Park produced a large number of football specials, as previously mentioned, and 27th April 1963 will always be remembered as the day that the West Midlands was invaded by Bulleid Pacifics. In this scene, which is much more typical of the 'South Western' main line from London Waterloo, two Pacifics are seen approaching Handsworth and Smethwick station with empty stock workings *en route* to Birmingham Snow Hill where they would have collected home-going Southampton supporters. On the right is 'West Country' Class No.34042 *Dorchester* hauling a motley collection of coaches, including BR Standard, Bulleid and Maunsell designs. On the other track, in the distance, is 'Battle of Britain' Class No.34088 *213 Squadron* powering a similar working. Sadly, none of the Southampton fans would have been smiling because their team was beaten by Manchester United who went on to win the Cup. At least they could console themselves with a long journey home with steam! *J J Smith / Bluebell Railway Museum*

A 'King' in the Black Country. Between Birmingham and Wolverhampton the former GWR line threaded one of the most heavily industrialised areas in Great Britain, a continuous jumble of factories, collieries, steelworks and foundries which probably account for Handsworth and Smethwick station's soot blackened main building just visible above the first coach of the train. The 2.10pm Paddington to Birkenhead (Woodside) is depicted passing through with 'King' Class 4-6-0 No.6022 *King Edward III* in charge on 28th May 1960. *R C Riley*

The scene is Handsworth Junction on 8th June 1964 with Stanier Class 8F No.48475 running 'light engine' from the West Bromwich direction towards Birmingham. In this photograph, full of interest, the remains of the former station named 'The Hawthorns Halt' may be glimpsed. Opened on Christmas Day 1931 the halt had four platforms, two on the tightly-curved Stourbridge line, one of which is visible on the left of the shot, and two on the West Bromwich line, both of which can just be discerned behind the locomotive. The name of the halt suggests that it provided access to a green Black Country oasis consisting of acres of parkland which was a refuge for ramblers but in fact it gave access to West Bromwich Albion's football ground. The halt was closed from 27th April 1968. After years of disuse following closure on 6th March 1972 the Birmingham to Wolverhampton line via West Bromwich was reopened (as far as Priestfield) as the Midland Metro tram line in 1999. *Tony Sullivan*

When Wednesbury station was constructed in the 1850s (it was renamed Wednesbury Central in 1950) it was probably an attractive building with red brick and creamy cornerstones plus other embellishments, but years of exposure to the polluted atmosphere of the West Midlands took its toll and by the early 1960s it was covered in soot. In this picture an unidentified, southbound van train passes through the station hauled by 'County' Class 4-6-0 No.1004 *County of Somerset* on 28th May 1960. *R C Riley*

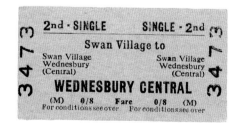

Wolverhampton was a veritable battleground between a number of railway companies and the disputes, legal battles and rulings by Parliament at various times would be sufficient to fill a large volume. On 3rd August 1846 Parliament gave authorisation for construction of a line between Birmingham and Wolverhampton via Tipton, promoted by the Birmingham, Wolverhampton & Stour Valley Railway Company; this company was soon absorbed into the LNWR. The Shrewsbury & Birmingham Railway (SBR) reached Wolverhampton in 1849, the line opening to a temporary station on 12th November. The SBR was given running powers over (what had become) the LNWR Stour Valley line but that company did everything in its power to prevent the SBR from exercising them and the situation turned really nasty on 7th July 1850 when a riot developed involving navvies employed by the SBR and LNWR. Police and soldiers marched to the scene to quell the disturbance and the protagonists did not quieten down until an injunction was obtained. After many bitter legal arguments over a number of years the SBR eventually started to run through from Wolverhampton High Level to Birmingham New Street on 4th February 1854, but on 14th November the Birmingham Wolverhampton & Dudley line (via Wednesbury) opened and the GWR, which had purchased the SBR, immediately diverted its trains to use the low level station at Wolverhampton. This station, jointly run with the Oxford Worcester & Wolverhampton Railway at first, was built with most of the facilities on the west side nearest the town, thus avoiding the risk to passengers when crossing the tracks, and the westernmost platform was initially used for both up and down services. The line from Birmingham was mixed gauge for a time but from 1st November 1864 all trains southwards to Snow Hill were worked on the standard gauge. Oxley viaduct, in the Wolverhampton suburbs, proved to be the most northerly point reached by the broad gauge, the GWR's ambition of reaching Merseyside having been thwarted. The removal of the broad gauge tracks presented the opportunity for the station to be remodelled in 1869 with separate up and down platforms, while another landmark was the building in 1899 of a carriage shed to the east of the station and diversion of the goods lines to run between the station and shed. In more recent times the station was well-known as a fascinating engine changing point for Paddington to Birkenhead expresses where 'King' class locomotives would be replaced on northbound trains by a smaller engine, the 'Kings' being prohibited north of Wolverhampton until a bridge was re-built at Shifnal in the mid-1950s. Sporadic steam workings to and from Shrewsbury/Chester continued until the withdrawal of the Birkenhead trains in March 1967, an event that left Wolverhampton Low Level with only a residual local service to Birmingham Snow Hill which, BR claimed at an inquiry in late 1966, would cost £917,400 to run over a projected five year period. BR went to great lengths to obtain ministerial consent to the withdrawal of these trains which survived until 6th March 1972, by which time the low level station had been largely converted to a parcels depot. It survived in this guise until 1981 but the station building still survives at the time of writing in private ownership. This picture of the main station building was taken from the approach road on a gloomy 5th November 1966. *Tommy Tomalin*

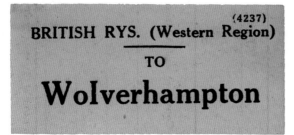

The Shrewsbury & Birmingham Railway established a locomotive repair works at Wolverhampton as early as 1849 and when the GWR took over Stafford Road works increased in importance, the first locomotive built there being a 2-2-2 which was out-shopped in 1859. The GWR undertook major improvements to the works which turned out 794 new locomotives before building work was transferred to Swindon in 1908; the shortage of land at Wolverhampton was a factor in this decision. The last engine to be built there was 2-6-2T No.4519 while the final Wolverhampton-built engine to remain in BR traffic was No.4507 which lasted until October 1963. Repair work at Stafford Road works continued, however, and even when the BR Modernisation Plan was announced in 1955 it was envisaged that the works would take on repairs to the new forms of traction. In 1959 310 locomotives were repaired and 183 boilers overhauled but a gradual decline followed and closure was announced on 22nd August 1963. The repair undertaken on 2800 Class 2-8-0 No.2859 proved to be the last, the locomotive leaving the works on 11th February 1964 in a blaze of publicity with TV cameras present. Just over a hundred years of history came to an end when the works was closed on 1st June 1964, regrettably rendering 500 men redundant. Engines released from the works often found themselves pressed into service on local duties before returning to their home shed and one of the most unusual instances occurred on 21st January 1961 when 1500 Class 0-6-0PT No.1507, an Old Oak Common engine normally employed on empty stock workings from Paddington, found itself working the 10.15am Wolverhampton (Low Level) to Leamington Spa via Worcester and Stratford-upon-Avon! This interior view of the works was taken on 13th March 1960. *W Potter / Kidderminster Railway Museum*

The most impressive and best-loved locomotives that worked the Wolverhampton to London trains were undoubtedly the former GWR 'King' Class 4-6-0s, one of the most powerful express passenger types in Great Britain. In this illustration No.6020 *King Henry IV*, in exemplary condition, sits outside Stafford Road shed on an unknown date awaiting its next turn of duty. The history of Stafford Road shed closely mirrors that of the works and its history can be traced back to 1854. A four-road broad gauge shed is understood to have been the first on the site, followed by a roundhouse for standard gauge engines that opened in 1860. In 1874/75 two further roundhouses were constructed and later a four-road straight shed specifically for rail motors. The site offered no further room for expansion and the structures mentioned above continued in use, in extremely decrepit condition, until the shed's closure on 9th September 1963. The shed's allocation was transferred on paper to the nearby Oxley depot but in reality most of its stud of thirteen 'Castle' Class engines remained in store there together with three other locomotives. The coaling stage continued in use at weekends for a while to ease congestion at Oxley. The buildings stood derelict for a couple of years until razed to the ground in mid-1966.
John Tarrant / Kidderminster Railway Museum

BIRMINGHAM (SNOW HILL) TO WOLVERHAMPTON (LOW LEVEL)

A rather grimy 'Modified Hall' Class locomotive, No.6987 *Shervington Hall* is seen approaching the Wolverhampton suburbs with an up train some time in the late 1950s. In the background, beyond the end of the viaduct, part of the huge Oxley marshalling yard can be discerned. Note the old coach body, adjacent to the signal box, which appears at first sight to be suspended in mid-air. It should be noted that the last three pictures in this section were taken a mile or so north of Wolverhampton (Low Level) station. *Mike Esau*

The section of line from Ashchurch to Birmingham was originally part of the Birmingham & Gloucester Railway (BGR), the beginnings of which can be traced back to 1832 when a possible route was surveyed by Isambard Kingdom Brunel. During the following year two proposed routes were evaluated by the directors of the BGR who decided in favour of the line over the Lickey incline and rejected Brunel's idea of a route further to the east which would have avoided that natural obstacle. The Lickey incline, the steepest gradient on any British main line, was not the only drawback to the course chosen because it by-passed towns such as Stourbridge and Dudley, not to mention Worcester, which some people said would have produced considerable revenue. Alas, the BGR was short of capital and the relatively high cost of land in those towns would probably have thwarted any plans to serve them. The BGR took

some time to raise sufficient money to start construction but at least Parliament did not stand in its way, the Bill being passed at first submission. Rather than start work in the Birmingham area as the company's title suggested, construction actually commenced at the southern end of the route with the 31 miles-long stretch between Cheltenham and Bromsgrove opening on 24th June 1840 while a further section southwards to Gloucester opened on 4th November 1840. The stretch north of Bromsgrove was brought into use in stages with the last section to Camp Hill, Birmingham, being opened on 17th December of the same year. Later BGR trains ran to Curzon Street station which was also served by the London & Birmingham Railway. The BGR became part of the Midland Railway (MR) on 3rd August 1846. In 1864 a direct connection was laid between St. Andrew's and Landor Street junctions, south of Saltley, that facilitated through running between Derby and Bristol. MR trains were still unable to enter New Street station, however, and through coaches were attached or detached as necessary at Camp Hill or Saltley. The Birmingham West Suburban Railway, which ran from King's Norton and Lifford to Granville Street in the city centre, opened in stages in 1876. In 1881 the MR obtained an Act authorising the doubling and extension of this line from Church Road Junction (just south of Five Ways station) to New Street where the MR platforms were brought into use on 8th February 1885. Initially some MR cross-country trains used the LNWR side of the station for passengers' convenience but caused congestion and from 1889 were confined to the MR side of the station. The final operation resulting from the MR's arrival in the city was the construction of its own independent, double track access from Landor Street Junction to Proof House Junction; this was completed in May 1896. In this picture Stanier Class 5MT No.44806 is seen approaching Ashchurch station with an up express on 22nd July 1961. *Charles Firminger*

A gem of a picture taken at Defford, between Ashchurch and Bromsgrove, on 23rd April 1962 with a vintage LMS oil lamp indicating the way to the station; the village can be seen on the horizon. The train service published in the 1961 summer timetable reveals a very sparse service principally designed for workpeople and unsuspecting travellers who just missed a train could be faced with a four hour wait, so BR obligingly displayed the local Midland Red bus timetable to assist prospective passengers in distress. Readers could be forgiven for thinking at first sight that this tiny wayside station had two signal boxes but, in reality, the box nearer the camera had been positioned on a substantial brick foundation and converted to an out-house. The 'real' signal box, which was in use until May 1964, is visible in the background on the left of the picture. Defford station closed on 4th January 1965 when local services along the line were abandoned so a Midland Red timetable really would have been essential reading for those villagers dependent on public transport. *John Langford*

Opposite: A new signal box with patterned brickwork was built at Ashchurch in the late 1950s and opened on 27th July 1958; it was photographed against a delightful rural backdrop on 22nd July 1961. At the time of its construction Ashchurch signal box controlled a moderately busy country junction station but the closure of the two branch lines that radiated from there rendered it superfluous and, after a very short existence, the box was closed from 17th February 1969. The station itself did not last much longer, being shut down from 15th November 1971. The cattle pen and wooden-bodied coal wagon in the foreground add to this appealing country scene. The main line tracks go straight ahead across the picture towards Birmingham while those curving away led to Evesham, a route that was deprived of its passenger trains from 17th June 1963. The tracks nearest to the camera are those that formerly ran to Great Malvern via Upton-on-Severn. A particularly interesting facet of operations at Ashchurch in bygone days was a flat crossing north of the station that enabled trains to run direct from Evesham to Upton-on-Severn but this facility was not greatly used in more recent times and was removed in 1957. *Charles Firminger*

Steam enthusiasts who enjoyed non-stop action were drawn to Bromsgrove where something always seemed to happening – if there was a lull in activity on the main line the Lickey bankers would either be crossing over from the down line or raising steam at the coal stage between turns. In this picture, taken almost half a mile south of Bromsgrove station on 20th April 1957, there is certainly a lot going on to entertain a bystander. In the far distance a huge column of smoke indicates that a goods train is setting off up the incline towards Blackwell, while an unidentified 4F Class 0-6-0 waits patiently for the 'road' beside Bromsgrove South signal box. Note the location of the turntable, a long way from the engine shed, the latter being hidden away among the cluster of buildings in the middle of the photograph on the right hand side of the main line. The locomotive nearest to the camera, standing at the coal stage, is Class 3F 0-6-0T No.47502, the class being commonly known as 'Jinties'. The coaling facilities were rudimentary in the extreme and latterly consisted of a conveyor mounted on a platform of sleepers. Staff were protected from the elements by a 'home made' canopy while the installation was gas lit, but there was presumably no protection from swirling coal dust. Romance of the steam age – forget it! *R C Riley*

Between Bromsgrove and Blackwell lies the infamous 1 in 37 Lickey incline, the steepest main line gradient in Great Britain, and during the steam era it presented a formidable challenge to enginemen. A small fleet of locomotives, dedicated for assisting northbound trains, was maintained at Bromsgrove shed and for many years Fowler-designed 0-10-0 No.58100, universally known as 'Big Bertha', undertook banking duties until it was withdrawn in 1956. It was replaced by BR Standard Class 9F No.92079 which, like its predecessor, was fitted with a large headlight to assist when drawing up to the rear of a train in darkness. The banking engines operated from a small wooden coaling stage on the opposite side of the main line to Bromsgrove shed and when this picture was taken there on 1st October 1961 No.92234 was assigned for banking work with two pannier tank engines, Nos.9429 and 8402, similarly employed. In the early 1960s the introduction of diesel locomotives caused a reduction in the number of trains requiring assistance and the banking duties themselves were turned over to diesel operation in September 1964. *Tommy Tomalin*

A couple of nicely cleaned veterans, Class 3F 0-6-0 Nos.43762 and 43186, pose outside Bromsgrove shed on 20th April 1957. The depot at Bromsgrove was originally built by the Birmingham & Gloucester Railway when the line opened in 1840; it was constructed primarily to house and maintain locomotives employed on banking duties on the Lickey incline. The locomotive shed occupied the same site as a much larger wagon works and was surrounded by a spring and machine shop, wagon repair shed plus a paint shop. An unusual feature of Bromsgrove shed was the location of the turntable which in 1892 was moved to a site about 640yds south of the shed building. During the BR regime some money was spent on improvements as evidenced here by the relatively new frontage to the shed building. The famous 0-10-0 banking locomotive, No.58100, spent its entire working life at Bromsgrove. The shed was closed from 27th September 1964 when steam traction was displaced on banking duties.
R C Riley

The battle up the Lickey! While the Lickey incline undoubtedly provided some of the most dramatic scenes of raw steam power in Great Britain as locomotives were worked to their limit on the 1 in 37 gradient, some enginemen were tempted to let the banking engines take most of the strain. This illustration shows the 8.30am Cardiff General to Newcastle upon Tyne train ascending the bank with 'Black Five' No.44753 piloting 'Jubilee' No.45664 *Nelson* on an overcast 22nd July 1961. Strangely, neither locomotive at the front of the train seems to making much of an effort and, indeed, both are 'blowing off' so they could not have been short of steam! The banking engines on this occasion were 9400 Class 0-6-0PTs Nos.8401 and 8402, both of which seem to be pushing mightily at the rear of the train. The pannier tank engines, drafted in by the Western Region in 1958, were probably considered to be intruders at Bromsgrove. *Charles Firminger*

The Lickey incline has always been a magnet for photographers but few could have been fortunate enough to capture a BR Standard Class 9F 2-10-0 with a former Crosti boiler climbing the bank with a train of Southern Region coaches in tow. What an absolutely amazing combination! The locomotive, No.92024, was hauling a Bournemouth West to Nottingham relief and this picture was taken on 18th August 1962; the banking engines were Nos.8405 and 9430. *Neville Simms*

We've made it! After more than two miles of climbing at a gradient of 1 in 37¾, during which their train would have ascended 307ft, the crew of Stanier 'Jubilee' 4-6-0 No.45566 *Queensland* have the summit in their sights and can now take it relatively easy as they head towards Birmingham. Two banking engines are clearly pushing mightily at the rear of the train in this scene which was recorded on 8th July 1961. The number of bankers used on each train was strictly controlled and depended on its weight and, in the late 1950s, the maximum unassisted load for a 'Jubilee' or BR Standard Class 5MT was 90 tons. Locomotives of this power range were permitted to take 270 tons with one banking locomotive but trains exceeding this figure were required to have assistance from two 'Jinty' 0-6-0T bankers or Bromsgrove shed's resident Class 9F 2-10-0. Three 'Jinties' were stipulated if the load exceeded 350 tons, or one 'Jinty' and the Class 9F. The drivers of northbound trains warned of their banking requirements by the number of whistles sounded as they passed Stoke Works Junction, where the signalman passed on the advice to Bromsgrove South signal box. One wonders what would have happened if any particularly confident drivers decided to ignore the regulations and 'have a go' with a heavy load only to grind to an embarrassing halt halfway up the bank! It should be noted that, by the time of this photograph, 'Jinties' had been replaced on banking duties by Class 9400 pannier tank locomotives. *Edwin Wilmshurst*

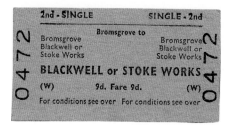

ASHCHURCH TO BIRMINGHAM (NEW STREET)

The regulations governing up trains on the Lickey incline were understandably rigorously controlled to avoid trains stalling and blocking a very busy main line, but the crews of down trains also had to obey the special safety rules. Goods trains were obliged to stop at Blackwell to have a proportion of their brakes pinned down and thereafter were restricted to 11mph on the descent. Passenger trains had to slow down to 10mph through Blackwell station and not exceed 27mph when descending the incline; a 10mph restriction applied over the curve into Bromsgrove station. In this picture Class 4F 0-6-0 No.44263 is shown proceeding gingerly down the bank from Blackwell station with a southbound unfitted goods working in the early 1960s. *John Tarrant / Kidderminster Railway Museum*

Train spotting really took off as a hobby after the Second World War when definitive information about BR locomotives became readily available. Here a group of young lads look southwards as B1 Class locomotive No.61167, hauling the 8.50am SO Paignton-Leeds City holiday train, approaches Barnt Green on 22nd July 1961. Interestingly, this train was booked to run non-stop between Bristol (dep. 11.50am), where the B1 presumably took over, and Derby (arr. 3.28pm). Barnt Green station on a summer Saturday must have been an ideal location for young spotters with a constant procession of holiday trains on the main line from the Midlands and north of England to the west country. Perhaps there was even the occasional bonus of a 'double header' – absolute magic! *Charles Firminger*

A southbound stopping passenger train, hauled by Stanier Class 5MT 4-6-0 No.44814, 'blows off' impatiently before leaving Barnt Green station; this picture is thought to have been taken in the late 1950s. The line to Redditch is out of sight on the right, having diverged from the main Gloucester route on a very tight curve beyond the footbridge which can just be discerned. The bracket signal on the left refers to up trains on the main line while the signal on the right of the picture controls those on the line from Redditch; the latter indicates that the line is clear for a train off the Redditch route to proceed towards Birmingham on the fast line. The lower signal arm on both brackets refers to movements along the slow line to Birmingham. *John Tarrant / Kidderminster Railway Museum*

A shot of the interior of Bournville shed taken in the late 1950s. The locomotive nearest to the camera is Johnson-designed Class 2F 0-6-0 No.58261, a genuine 'old timer' whose history dated back to 1892 when it was built by Dubs & Co. in Glasgow; it survived in traffic until January 1960. The depot was a standard MR roundhouse and opened in 1895, comparatively late compared to other sheds in the West Midlands area; it stood alongside the Birmingham West Suburban line. The shed was equipped with a 50ft turntable, a single coal road and was built to cater for an expected upsurge in traffic which never fully materialised, so the shed always seemed to have spare capacity. This encouraged its use for locomotive storage and long lines of silent engines could often be found slumbering beside the shed building. In 1924 the allocation stood at a mere 15 locomotives but had risen to 29 by 1945 following the introduction of several 2-6-4Ts on suburban services. In 1956 an engine fell into the turntable pit, damaging the turntable to the extent that it had to be sent away to Swindon for repair. The depot was closed on 14th February 1960 and it is recorded that the last locomotive to leave under its own steam was 'Black Five' No.44843. *John Tarrant / Kidderminster Railway Museum*

The 12.15pm from Birmingham New Street to Worcester, headed by BR Standard Class 5MT No.73031, accelerates through Selly Oak station on 2nd June 1962; the fireman has clearly just put a few more shovelfuls of coal onto the fire, doubtless pleasing the photographer. Passengers were left in no doubt when they arrived at Selly Oak because in addition to large nameboards each ornate gas lamp standard was fully kitted out with a BR 'sausage' sign displaying the station's name. Note the neat buildings and generally tidy state of the station which was presumably manned during the busiest periods. *Tommy Tomalin*

When leaving Birmingham New Street towards Selly Oak the first intermediate station is Five Ways and in this picture Stanier Class 5MT No.45447 is seen passing the station's abandoned platforms with a Worcester-bound train on 7th March 1964. The train has just emerged from the last of a series of tunnels between New Street and Five Ways and the locomotive would have been working hard up the 1 in 80 gradient that prevails at this point. Five Ways station has an interesting history, having been closed temporarily from 2nd October 1944 and then permanently in November 1950. This inner city station made a comeback when the Cross City suburban service was introduced, re-opening from 8th May 1978. *Neville Simms*

The Midland Railway's platforms at Birmingham New Street were opened, as previously mentioned, in 1885 but by the time this photograph was taken on 30th May 1964 the premises had become very dirty and run-down, and rebuilding of the entire station was envisaged. This picture certainly illustrates how railway stations have altered over the years; note the old fashioned barrows laden with mail bags and ancient departure indicators consisting of a manually operated clock face and finger boards. Surely, the last mentioned could not have been the original equipment dating from 1885? The footbridge spanned the entire station and was stipulated in the original Act authorising its construction; this stated that 'a public footpath was to be open continuously by day and night and lighted'. The posters and advertisements also give an insight into the 1960s era, note the 'Ask the Man from Cooks' advertisement and BR poster promoting their 'Door to Door Container Service to Ireland'. Amazingly for a main line, city centre station the uninviting platforms were still gas-lit, but all of this was soon to be swept away by a 1960s concrete monstrosity that many people considered to be worse. *Tommy Tomalin*

A scene at the western end of Birmingham New Street station with Ivatt Class 4MT 2-6-0 No.43027 standing on the middle road between platforms seven and eight; this picture was taken on 27th June 1958. The engine is 'blowing off' and was presumably on station pilot duty. On the right a couple of tank locomotives are partially visible; that nearest to the camera appears to be a Fowler-designed engine while the other one seems to be a Stanier type. Note the rather dainty lower quadrant signals. *Tony Sullivan*

Stanier's finest? 'Princess Coronation' Class Pacific No.46240 *City of Coventry* may have seen better days but, even so, it adds a much needed splash of colour to the unbelievably squalid surroundings of Birmingham New Street station, seen here in this scene from 1963. Sadly, time was running out for *City of Coventry* because it was one of the 18 surviving members still in service when a mass slaughter of this celebrated class occurred in September 1964. Rather strangely, this shot was taken on the old 'Midland' side of New Street station and not on the 'North Western' side where locomotives of this class would normally be expected to appear – perhaps No.46240 was working some sort of special train. *Courtesy RCTS Photo Archive*

The importance of Saltley shed can be gauged by the fact that in 1954 the depot had an almost unbelievable total of 191 locomotives on its books. Basic accommodation for locomotives had been provided by the Birmingham & Derby Junction Railway as far back as 1839 but a proper building was not built until 1854. In 1867 a new shed was opened on a different site that had room for expansion and a further building was commissioned alongside it in 1876; both were roundhouses. In 1900 a third roundhouse, much larger than its predecessors, was provided. Coal and ash plants were installed by the LMSR in 1936 and all three roundhouses were rebuilt by BR. Saltley was predominantly a freight depot which for many years had a huge allocation of LMSR 0-6-0s, but these were slowly displaced by more modern classes and in this shot dating from March 1960 the variety of classes on view include LMSR Class 5MT 4-6-0s and 8F 2-8-0s plus a BR Standard 9F and WD 2-8-0. The shed was closed on 6th March 1967. *W Potter / Kidderminster Railway Museum*

The year 1966 was the last full year of Saltley shed as an operational steam depot and here five Class 8F 2-8-0s huddle around one of the its turntables on 17th July 1966. One can almost smell that irresistible aroma of sulphur, steam and hot oil. *Neville Simms*

The fireman of Class 8F No.48604 appears to be wearing a knotted hankerchief, a cheap and, hopefully, very effective method of keeping coal dust out of his hair; one wonders whether this type of headgear was officially approved in the BR regulations. The 8F was working an eastbound goods train through Bromford Bridge station on 21st June 1962. This station was used solely by racegoers, the course being adjacent to the line, and this may account for its very dilapidated state; note the wooden platforms. Three years to the day after this picture was taken the last meeting took place at Bromford Bridge racecourse and the station was closed a week later on 28th June 1965. The large Nechells power station cooling towers are in the background. *Tony Sullivan*

Ashchurch station is the setting for this picture of former GWR 5700 Class 0-6-0PT No.7788 waiting to leave at the head of the 9.40am to Tewkesbury on 13th May 1961. Note the initials on the tank side! The main station building was behind the photographer. *John Langford*

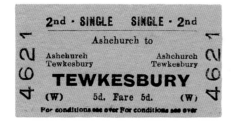

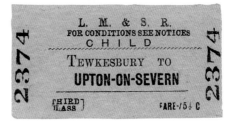

The Birmingham & Gloucester Railway opened a 1¾ miles-long branch from Ashchurch to Tewkesbury on 21st July 1840, the branch apparently being worked by horses until 1844. The line onwards to Great Malvern was proposed by the Tewkesbury & Malvern Railway and opened to traffic on 16th May 1864, the local company becoming part of the Midland Railway in 1877. Business was far from brisk on the northern section of the line above Upton-on-Severn and it is recorded that a maximum of five weekday trains was advertised in the late 1920s, but this had been reduced to three by 1949. The inevitable closure came on 1st December 1952, that part of the line being closed completely from that date. Services continued, however, on the link from Ashchurch to Upton-on-Severn via Tewkesbury but the service to and from Upton in the early 1960s was very sparse, but was supplemented by a few short workings to Tewkesbury. The 7¼ miles-long line was closed on 14th August 1961, the last train from Ashchurch to Upton being formed of two coaches packed to the gunwales with local people taking their last (and, in some cases, no doubt their first) trip over the line; motive power was Class 3F 0-6-0 No.43754. When it returned detonators sounded a noisy farewell at Tewkesbury, where the mayor was in attendance, and its arrival back at Ashchurch was filmed by television cameras. In this portrait of Tewkesbury station taken on 13th May 1961 5700 Class 0-6-0PT No.7788 is seen awaiting departure with the 11.10am train to Ashchurch, the return working of the train seen in the previous picture. *John Langford*

Tewkesbury had a small engine shed, a sub-shed of Gloucester Barnwood depot, which was located on the short goods line that formerly ran across the river Avon to serve two mills and the quay. In this picture 3F Class 0-6-0 No.43242, which had arrived on a goods working, can just be discerned in the background; the shed survived until 7th September 1962. Tewkesbury's first passenger station was also located on this line but it was closed in May 1864 when the branch from Ashchurch was extended to Great Malvern; the site of this station was still reasonably intact 90 years after closure. *John Langford*

Upton-on-Severn station's main building was richly decorated with patterned brickwork and also boasted a well-proportioned canopy which, unfortunately, is concealed by the train in this shot. The locomotive is 3F Class 0-6-0 No.43754 which, as previously mentioned, hauled the very last passenger train on the branch in August 1961. Goods traffic continued on the branch for almost a further two years after passenger trains ceased, being withdrawn from 1st July 1963. In 1946 the LMSR clearly considered that this rural backwater had a reasonable future and invested in a new signal box to replace the existing cabin that was presumably dilapidated. The new box lasted just over 12 years, being closed from 20th July 1958. This illustration shows the 5.10pm from Ashchurch after arrival on 22nd July 1961, less than a month before services were withdrawn.
Charles Firminger

| Table 171 | UPTON-ON-SEVERN, TEWKESBURY and ASHCHURCH |
| | WEEK DAYS ONLY (Second class only) |

Miles		S am	E am	am	am	pm	pm	pm	pm	Miles		am	E am	S am	S am	pm	pm	pm
—	Upton-on-Severn .. dep	7 37	7 57	..	..	1 30	..	..	5 45	—	Ashchurch .... dep	8 35	9 25	940	1130	2620	5 10	6 20
2	Ripple	7 42	8 3	..	..	1 34	..	..	5A57	1¾	Tewkesbury .. { arr	8 40	9 30	945	1135	2625	5 15	6 25
5½	Tewkesbury { arr	7 48	8 9	..	..	1 42	..	..	6 3		{ dep	..	..	..	1137	..	5 17	..
5½	{ dep	7 50	8 11	8850	1110	..	1 43	4 156	6	5¾	Ripple	..	..	..	1147	..	5 25	..
7½	Ashchurch .. arr	7 55	8 16	8855	1115	..	1 48	4 206	11	7½	Upton-on-Severn .. arr	..	..	..	1152	..	5 29	..

| A Arr 5 49 pm | | E Except Saturdays | | S Saturdays only |
| B On Mondays to Fridays 3 minutes later | | G On Saturdays 5 minutes later | | |

Extract from Western Region Summer 1961 timetable

Like so many routes, the Barnt Green to Ashchurch via Evesham line was constructed in stages, the first section from Barnt Green to Redditch opening for passenger traffic on 19th September 1859. The Evesham & Redditch Railway was authorised in 1863 to close the gap between the towns and Evesham to Alcester was subsequently opened to passengers on 17th September 1866, while the last stretch on to Redditch carried its first passenger train on 4th May 1868. The MR had opened the Ashchurch to Evesham line to passengers on 1st October 1864 and this completed the loop between Barnt Green and Ashchurch. While the early history of the line is relatively straightforward the withdrawal of services south of Redditch in the 1960s is complicated due to the involvement of the Civil Engineer responsible for that particular section of line. The passenger service between Evesham and Redditch was withdrawn at short notice on 1st October 1962 because the Civil Engineer declared the track on the Broom Junction to Evesham section to be unsafe; buses replaced trains on the section affected. The Ashchurch to Redditch line had already been proposed for closure and the last train, comprising pannier tank locomotive No.3745 plus two coaches, ran between Ashchurch and Evesham only on Saturday 15th June 1963, the service being officially withdrawn two days later. Goods traffic continued on some sections of the route for a while afterwards, that on the Ashchurch to Evesham stretch running for the last time on 9th September 1963. The first station south of Barnt Green is Alvechurch which is depicted in this portrait, thought to date from the 1960s. *John Tarrant / Kidderminster Railway Museum*

Apart from Evesham, which was also served by trains on the Worcester to Paddington line, Redditch was the only major intermediate station on the Barnt Green to Ashchurch route and in this shot bunker-first Fowler-designed Class 4MT 2-6-4T No.42416 is seen arriving with the 2.55pm train to Ashchurch on 22nd July 1961. Four trains between Redditch and Ashchurch and vice versa were advertised on Mondays to Fridays in the summer 1961 timetable while on Saturdays an additional service was provided; the sparse service reflected the predominantly rural nature of the line. If any prospective passengers had been unlucky enough to miss the train depicted here they could console themselves with the prospect of a three hour wait for the next train which left at 6.00pm! *Charles Firminger*

Broom Junction was, perhaps, the most interesting intermediate station on the Redditch to Evesham section; the station is seen here in this picture taken on 22nd April 1962. Passenger facilities were unpretentious and consisted of a motley collection of buildings including an old coach body that presumably served as a waiting shelter. In former years Broom was the junction for the Stratford-upon-Avon and Midland Junction Railway (SMJR) cross-country line towards Towcester and Blisworth, this being a vital link for goods traffic especially during the Second World War when a south to east curve was laid. Passenger services on that line were early victims of rationalisation, however, those between Broom and Stratford-upon-Avon being withdrawn temporarily in 1947 (permanently from 23rd May 1949) while the remainder onwards to Blisworth lasted until 7th April 1952. Goods services along the SMJR branch from Broom Junction continued until 13th June 1960. Broom Junction station's principal function was as an interchange station, but despite losing this role it remained in use until the premature closure of the line south of Redditch. *John Langford*

The 6.30am train from Birmingham New Street to Ashchurch via Redditch, with Fowler 2-6-4T No.42400 in charge, is depicted at Broom Junction station on 13th May 1961. This train had a very leisurely schedule, taking more than two hours for the 43 miles-long journey, its progress being hampered by long waits at some stations; it is waiting to cross the 7.14am *ex*-Ashchurch with No.42422 in charge. *John Langford*

Salford Priors was a pretty, well-maintained wayside station that had, among other attributes, an exceptional variety of chimney pots! The substantial stationmaster's house had perhaps been rented out to a fortunate BR employee by the time this portrait was taken in April 1962 and the station was doubtless unstaffed. Note the old LMSR 'hawkseye' station nameboard, which appears to have been recently repainted, and set of dainty platform oil lamps. The goods yard comprised two sidings, one of which was a loop off the 'main' line. *John Langford*

LONDON MIDLAND AND SCOTTISH
RAILWAY COMPANY.　　**M.R.**　P. F. 70.
　　　　　　　　　　　　　　　R 2a.

Salford Priors

The signalman at Harvington station stands in classic pose as he waits to hand over the token to the fireman of Ivatt Class 4MT 2-6-0 No.43046 which was working a northbound passenger train in the early 1960s. The signal box there controlled a passing loop, being strategically positioned halfway between Broom Junction and Evesham. *John Spencer Gilks*

The former LMSR station at Evesham was adjacent to the GWR station which, as previously stated, was on the Worcester to Paddington line and was, therefore, likely to have been the much busier of the two. The LMSR premises were enhanced by an attractive canopy on the northbound platform and the station building appears to have been kept in a tidy condition by the staff who, after all, had plenty of time between trains! Note the scales and barrows, pieces of equipment that were absolutely indispensible for the efficient running of any station at that time. One wonders how much business was done at the W H Smith bookstall if, indeed, it was still open. This picture was taken looking eastwards on 8th June 1962 at the height of summer... *Tommy Tomalin*

...but in the depths of winter Evesham station, carpeted in snow, took on an entirely different appearance. This shot depicts former GWR Class 5700 pannier tank locomotive No.8743 waiting to leave with the 12.24pm to Ashchurch on 12th January 1963 during a period of arctic weather that gripped Great Britain for some weeks. *Edwin Wilmshurst*

The direct line from Birmingham to Stratford-upon-Avon proved to be the last major addition to the GWR's system in the West Midlands. The GWR's 'Holiday Haunts' publication misleadingly stated that Shakespeare's country had been further opened up by this line and that it represented the final link in the company's Birmingham to Bristol route. In reality, the principal purpose of the route was to serve the scattered communities located in that pleasantly rural part of Warwickshire which was barely ten miles from the centre of Birmingham. The first proposals for such a line were made by local landowners who wanted an independent route between Birmingham and Stratford; they received parliamentary approval on 25th August 1894. It was envisaged that the North Warwickshire line would run 24 miles from Moor Street to Stratford. The plans of the original promoters were destined to be unfulfilled, however, and the grandly named Birmingham North Warwickshire and Stratford-upon-Avon Railway Company had to settle for a route that would diverge from the GWR just south of Tyseley station which put paid to their idea of a completely independent route. Predictably, the local company failed to attract the necessary capital and the GWR stepped in, taking over from 30th July 1900. A revision of the route was also made at the southern end where it met the GWR's existing Hatton to Stratford line at Bearley. The North Warwickshire route opened to goods traffic on 9th December 1907 and to passengers on 1st July 1908. The line became part of the GWR's route between Birmingham and Bristol via Winchcombe which was intended to rival the MR line connecting the two cities. The GWR failed to encourage many commuters and after the Second World War stringent planning controls frustrated further development and BR stated that the line was running at a substantial loss, seeking closure from 5th May 1969. Five local authorities took their case for retention to the High Court and in 1970 the West Midlands Passenger Transport Authority threw the route a lifeline, offering a subsidy for that part of the route in their territory, and later all threats of closure were removed – what a turnaround. Like other suburban routes in the Birmingham area few colour pictures of steam operations on the Tyseley to Stratford-upon-Avon line appear to have been taken, perhaps due to the early introduction of diesel units on most services, but here is a photograph of a Locomotive Club of Great Britain rail tour passing Earlswood Lakes station behind BR Standard 'Britannia' Pacific No.70004 *William Shakespeare* on 12th November 1966. *John Spencer Gilks*

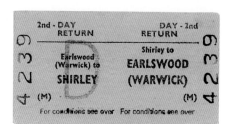

BIRMINGHAM (SNOW HILL) TO STRATFORD-UPON-AVON

Henley-in-Arden was the most important station on the North Warwickshire Line and originally consisted of three platforms, the main station buildings being on the southbound platform. The other platform was an island, with one face for northbound services while the track serving the outer face was used by terminating trains from Birmingham. The latter had a loop to enable locomotives to easily run-round their train before returning northwards. The signal box was strategically positioned on the up side, north of the station, doubtless to provide signalmen with a good view of run-round operations. This station, however, was not the first to serve Henley-in-Arden because in 1894 a short, three miles-long branch was opened from Kingswood (later Lapworth) but passenger services ceased in 1915 so it was very short-lived. This branch was connected to the North Warwickshire line by a goods-only spur which continued in use until the end of December 1962 so it outlasted the original passenger line by a mere 47 years! This view of Henley-in-Arden station, looking southwards towards Stratford-upon-Avon, was taken on 4th July 1963.
Lens of Sutton Association

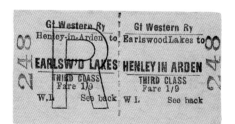

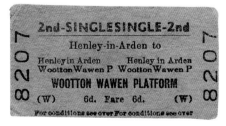

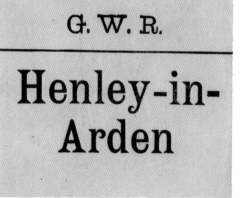

BIRMINGHAM (SNOW HILL) TO STRATFORD-UPON-AVON

The 7.05am SO train from Leamington Spa to Stratford-upon-Avon pauses at Wilmcote on 29th August 1964; motive power is provided by 2251 Class 0-6-0 No.2211, one of a number of these locomotives based at Leamington Spa shed. Wilmcote station was lovingly maintained by its staff, the appearance of the platforms being considerably improved by a colourful rambling rose bush, flower beds and white-washed plant pots. Despite the relatively early hour there is a small group of passengers on the platform. Wilmcote station is at the top of a short, sharp 1 in 75 bank from Stratford-upon-Avon and after departure from there the line makes a gentle descent for a couple of miles before climbing continuously for almost ten miles on a 1 in 150 gradient until Earlswood Lakes station is reached, so in steam days working this route was quite a challenge for engine crews working a heavy northbound train. *Neville Simms*

3rd-SINGLE SINGLE-3rd		
	Stratford-upon-Avon to	
Stratford u Avon		Stratford u Avon
S00		S.00
Wilmcote		Wilmcote
	WILMCOTE	
(W) 6d	FARE	6d (W)
For conditions see over		For conditions see over

The Oxford Worcester & Wolverhampton Railway (OWWR) was largely promoted by Worcestershire businessmen who wished to break the London & Birmingham Railway's (LBR) monopoly on goods traffic between the Black Country, London and the ports in the south of England through which Midland manufacturers despatched their goods to the rest of the world. The 89 miles-long route was planned to stretch, as its title suggests, from Wolvercote Junction, just north of Oxford, via Worcester, Droitwich, Kidderminster and Dudley to Wolverhampton where a link with the Grand Junction Railway was envisaged. The promoters obtained an Act on 4th August 1845 following a battle with the LBR who had proposed a line from Tring to Wolverhampton via the Vale of Evesham. The OWWR had the backing of the GWR which had hopes of extending the broad gauge to the West Midlands as part of a cherished dream of reaching the river Mersey. The OWWR, however, was destined to have a stormy history and things went awry right from the start when Brunel grossly underestimated construction costs and was forced to increase the original figure of £1m by two and a half times. Even worse was to come because construction of the whole line had been started at the same time and the money ran out before even a small section had been finished. A further blow to shareholders was the GWR's purchase of two West Midlands railway companies that provided a shorter route from there to the Capital. The first two stretches of the OWWR to be finished were both in the Worcester area and these opened in the early 1850s, the company being keen to tap the traffic to Droitwich which was a rapidly developing Victorian spa town. Further sections of route were brought into use on a piecemeal basis and a major milestone was reached on 4th June 1853 when the 40½ miles-long stretch between Evesham and Wolvercote was opened. There was trouble on this section when troops had to be summoned to Mickleton, near Honeybourne, when a contractor, who had been sacked by Brunel, refused to leave the site and Brunel assembled 2,000 navvies in support. There was a minor confrontation but the contractor fled and the troops were stood down. The last stage of the line to be finished was in the Black Country, from Stourbridge Junction to Wolverhampton via Dudley and Bilston and this section was opened throughout to goods traffic in April 1854 and to passenger trains on 1st July. The following July saw the commissioning of a short link to the LNWR at Bushbury Junction. Operations on the OWWR were plagued by unreliable locomotives which frequently failed, thus making a mockery of the timetable to the extent that the line was disparagingly known as the 'Old Worse and Worse'. The station nameboard in the middle of the picture immediately identifies the location of this photograph which depicts 5101 Class 2-6-2T No.4175 departing from the north end of the station on 1st June 1963. *R C Riley*

The OWWR opened its first shed at Worcester in 1852 and this consisted of two separate buildings, a three-road affair for passenger locomotives while the goods engines were accommodated in a four-road shed. The sheds were in a triangle north of Shrub Hill station and separated by a steeply graded industrial branch which dived under the Hereford line and crossed various roads to serve Hill, Evans & Co's vinegar factory. Officially, this branch was called the Lowesmoor Tramway but it was universally known as 'The Vinegar Branch'. Unloved, encrusted with grime and devoid of its name and smokebox number plate, former GWR 'Grange' Class 4-6-0 No.6819 *Highnam Grange* stands over an inspection pit at Worcester shed on 19th September 1965 – a truly depressing sight for any GWR enthusiast. No.6819 was taken out of traffic just a few weeks after this picture was taken. During most of its career *Highnam Grange* was probably kept in splendid condition with gleaming paintwork and a brightly polished copper capped chimney which were the hallmarks of GWR tradition. The Western Region had, however, trumpeted its intention to dispense with steam traction by the end of 1965 and the condition of the remaining steam locomotives had been allowed to degenerate to the state where most seemed to be kept going with string and a prayer, as exemplified here by the absolutely disgraceful condition of No.6819. Whatever happened to that traditional Great Western pride? Surprisingly, steam traction actually gained a new working at the start of the 1965 summer timetable, with the Hereford portion of the 3.15pm *ex*-Paddington being steam-worked from Worcester, a regular performer being No.7904 *Fountains Hall*. This turn, and an afternoon school train to Ledbury, were the last diagrammed steam passenger workings from the city and both succumbed to diesel traction at the end of August. *R C Riley*

The first station from Worcester travelling northwards was Fernhill Heath but that was closed from 5th April 1965, the following station being Droitwich Spa which is depicted here in this picture dating from 1961. Just north of Droitwich the line split, with one route leading to Bromsgrove and Birmingham New Street while the other tracks led to Kidderminster and Birmingham Snow Hill. The signal box adjacent to the junction is just visible beyond the road overbridge in this picture. The principal station building was on the southbound platform, the opposite platform being equipped merely with rather crude-looking waiting shelters. Judging by the condition of the lamp standards, the premises appear to have had electric lighting recently installed. As at so many stations, very tall telegraph poles towered above the tracks. *Lens of Sutton Association*

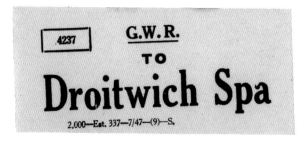

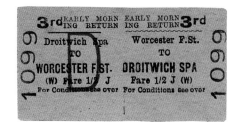

Kidderminster was blessed with a particularly distinctive station building designed with mock Tudor architecture; the station was opened on 1st May 1852. The frontage is seen here in this photograph taken on 18th March 1961 with the sunlit, mainly white building standing out against the dramatic, dark sky. Unfortunately, the building later suffered from dry rot and was demolished in 1968, being replaced by a characterless, utilitarian building. Today, the Severn Valley Railway's delightful terminal is a few yards away across the station forecourt. *John Langford*

Hagley station in the early 1960s, looking northwards, with a gentleman waiting patiently on a platform seat for a train towards Kidderminster. Both platforms have canopies, the larger of which is on the platform served by trains bound for Birmingham Snow Hill. During this period Hagley had quite a reasonable service of local trains from Worcester/Kidderminster to Birmingham. Hagley signal box can just be discerned beyond the road overbridge. Note that, as with other stations pictured in this book, very tall telegraph poles carried the wires well clear of the buildings. *Lens of Sutton Association*

The 12.25pm SO from Wolverhampton Low Level to Worcester Shrub Hill, with 5101 Class 2-6-2T No.4179 in charge, awaits departure from Dudley station on 2nd June 1962. The service between Wolverhampton and Dudley at that time was hardly frequent, consisting of about nine trains a day, the Monday to Friday timetable being clearly designed with workpeople in mind, there being very long gaps during the middle part of the day; most services terminated at either Stourbridge Junction or Worcester Shrub Hill. Other services, with an hourly frequency on weekdays, radiated from Dudley to Birmingham Snow Hill and Walsall, while trains also ran to Dudley Port and Old Hill. The last-mentioned service consisted of eight trains on Mondays to Fridays with just one or two on Saturdays. Sadly, all of these routes fell victim to the Beeching axe in the 1960s and on 6th July 1964 Dudley station closed its doors for the last time, leaving this Black Country town devoid of any rail passenger services apart from Dudley Port station on the Stour Valley line. The station site was subsequently cleared for redevelopment as a Freightliner terminal which opened on 6th November 1967. The Freightliner network was rationalised in the mid-1980s, however, with the result that the Dudley establishment was closed in 1989. *Charles Firminger*

WORCESTER (SHRUB HILL) TO WOLVERHAMPTON (LOW LEVEL)

A scene at Wolverhampton Low Level showing 5101 Class 2-6-2T No.4179 waiting to leave with the train seen in the previous picture. Despite its status as an important main line station where engines were routinely changed on Paddington to Birkenhead through trains, few pictures seem to have been taken at Wolverhampton Low Level, this being the only colour photograph of that location submitted for publication. No.4179 was, predictably perhaps, shedded at Wolverhampton Stafford Road shed at the time of this photograph. Built at Swindon in BR days, No.4179 was out-shopped in December 1949 and lasted in service until February 1965. *Charles Firminger*

The line from Stourbridge to Birmingham (Handsworth) was conceived by the Stourbridge Railway, incorporated on 14th June 1860, to build a 3½ miles-long branch from the OWWR at Stourbridge to Old Hill. Just over a year later the company was given authority to further extend to the Stour Valley line at Smethwick. The first section as far as Cradley opened on 1st April 1863 with the next stretch to Old Hill opening on 1st June 1866. The Stour Valley line was reached in April 1867 and the line continued to the GWR at Handsworth to enable through running into Snow Hill Station. Here, an unidentified westbound train, headed by 'Hall' Class 4-6-0 No.6922 *Burton Hall,* is depicted at Stourbridge Junction station on 17th April 1964. Stourbridge Junction was built at the turn of the century and consisted of two island platforms with the shuttle service from the Town station using the western face of the down platform. Stourbridge was a major traffic centre and the first engine shed there was a four-road affair dating from 1870 that had a chequered history, but it survived as a GWR diesel railcar depot and was refurbished by BR, not finally closing until July 1965. The principal steam shed was a massive 28-road roundhouse which was closed on 11th July 1966. *Roy Denison*

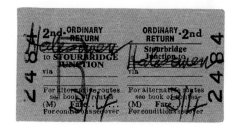

G. W. R.

STOURBRIDGE JUNCTION

A panoramic view of Lye taken from a road overbridge immediately west of the station, looking eastwards on 17th October 1963. The station still retained goods facilities at that time – note the wagons in the yard on the right of the picture. The eastbound platform has only a small waiting shelter while the rather modest main building is on the westbound platform. The signal box can just be identified beyond the footbridge. *Lens of Sutton Association*

Old Hill station was the junction for Dudley and in this view the 12.45pm to Dudley is seen awaiting departure behind an unidentified pannier tank locomotive on 25th February 1961. This photograph was taken on a Saturday and, incredibly, the 12.45pm was the last train of the day, the service clearly being arranged with work people in mind. Old Hill was also where passengers changed onto the Halesowen branch but regular public services were withdrawn as long ago as 5th December 1927 although workmen's trains continued until 1958. The station's nameboard was rather out of date and gave misleading information to passengers. Old Hill station marked the halfway point on the 1 in 51/81 climb from Cradley Heath and heavy trains were often assisted. *Edwin Wilmshurst*

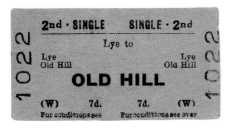

This picture was taken on 27th April 1963 when football specials ran from Southampton in connection with an FA Cup match at Villa Park and enthusiasts besieged Snow Hill station in order to witness the trains' passage through the station. Here, excited onlookers vie for the best photographic positions as Class 8F 2-8-0 No.48478, piloting Bulleid 'West Country' Pacific No.34009 *Lyme Regis,* approach the station. The 8F had been attached at Stourbridge to assist the Light Pacific up Old Hill bank with its 12-coach train. *J J Smith / Bluebell Railway Museum*

STOURBRIDGE JUNCTION TO BIRMINGHAM (SNOW HILL)

Birmingham Snow Hill station is the grand and unmistakable setting for this portrait of the 5.37pm train to Dudley waiting to depart on 20th April 1963 with 5101 Class 2-6-2T No.4167 in charge. Can any more be said? *Tommy Tomalin*

There is not too much 'romance' of the steam age on show in this picture of one of the football specials as it plunges into the smoky depths of Snow Hill tunnel on 27th April 1963; the locomotives are Bulleid 'West Country' Class Pacific No.34039 *Boscastle* and 8F Class 2-8-0 No.48417. It is interesting to note that even the 8F Class engine has been cleaned up especially for the occasion. *J J Smith / Bluebell Railway Museum*

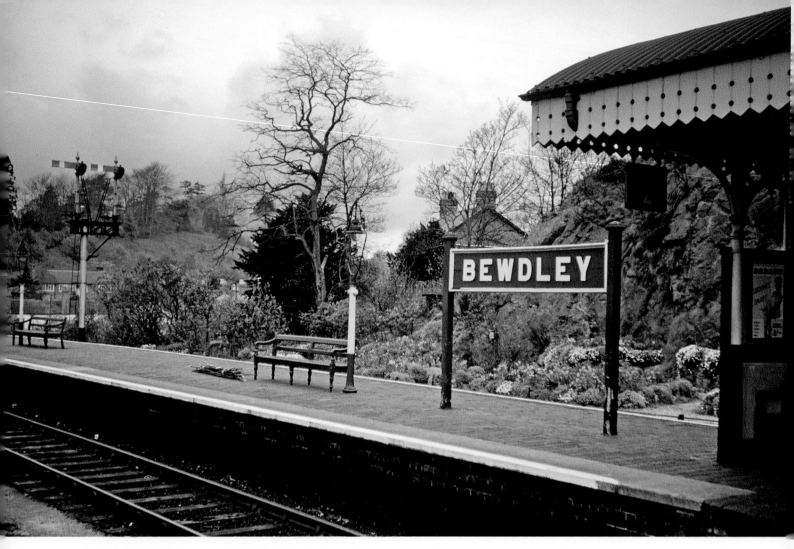

The preserved Severn Valley Railway is today probably the best-known, and certainly the most popular, section of railway in the area covered by this book. The line was originally part of the 39½ miles-long line between Hartlebury and Shrewsbury (Sutton Bridge Junction) which was authorised in 1853 but not opened until 1st February 1862. The route passed through the delightful town of Bewdley and on 1st June 1878 the GWR opened a short branch from there to nearby Kidderminster. The line may have been scenically attractive, but it did not serve any large intermediate traffic centres and the winter 1954/55 timetable lists a mere half a dozen trains each way on weekdays north of Bridgnorth though more were provided south thereof. Clearly such a line was vulnerable to closure in the harsh economic circumstances that faced BR in the 1960s and passenger trains between Bewdley and Shrewsbury ran for the last time on 8th September 1963. Subsequently the links from Bewdley to Kidderminster and Hartlebury also lost their regular passenger trains, both services being withdrawn from 5th January 1970. Today, the preserved Bewdley station is beautifully maintained but it also seems to have been well-kept in BR days, as illustrated here in this picture that dates from 1st April 1961.
John Langford

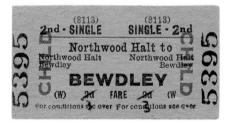

The 1.45pm Shrewsbury to Kidderminster train, with 8750 Class 0-6-0PT No.3788 in charge, pauses at Bridgnorth on 18th August 1962. This train took just over two hours to cover the 38¾ miles between the two towns including a 20-minute stop at Bridgnorth to take water and also cross a northbound train. Travelling on this train may have been a delightful experience for railway enthusiasts but, perhaps, a frustrating one for *bona fide* passengers. *Edwin Wilmshurst*

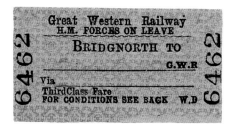

Extract from Western Region winter 1954/5 timetable

The old, tranquil days at Bridgnorth. An everyday scene at Bridgnorth station on 30th December 1960 showing a porter busy on the southbound platform, and the signalman observing movements from his box, as an empty coal train approaches behind 4300 Class 2-6-0 No.6388. A northbound goods working with 6100 Class 2-6-2T No.6128 in charge stands in the other platform and has the 'road' to leave now that the southbound train has cleared the single line section. Note that the goods shed appears to be busy. The ensuing years witnessed tumultuous events at Bridgnorth, which included the closure of the line by BR and the subsequent formation of the preservation society. The line reopened in 1970, and from modest beginnings the Severn Valley Railway has developed into one of the most successful tourist railways in Great Britain. *Hugh Ballantyne*

The branch line linking Bewdley and Woofferton Junction was a delight for railway aficionados but a headache for the railway authorities due to its rural nature and little prospect of developing traffic. The route was built on a piecemeal basis, the first section from Woofferton to Tenbury Wells being opened by the nominally independent Tenbury Railway on 1st August 1861 while the 14 miles-long stretch onwards to Bewdley opened on 13th August 1864. The second section was promoted by the appropriately named Tenbury & Bewdley Railway. The train service in the mid-1950s, when private car ownership was not as widespread as it is today, was a mere four daily trains in each direction between Woofferton Junction and Kidderminster on weekdays only. The timetable refers to 'limited accommodation', inferring that the trains were formed of GWR railcars. In addition to the four services mentioned there were two trains that ran to and from Tenbury Wells. The stretch west of Tenbury Wells was closed completely from 31st July 1961 from which date BR had hoped to shut the entire line, but in response to local pressure one train was retained on Mondays to Fridays Only between Tenbury Wells and Bewdley and return, mainly for the benefit of schoolchildren. This arrangement was on the basis that BR would withdraw it without further consultation after one year if usage failed to meet expectations. Predictably perhaps, the service was taken off exactly a year later but this made railway history because the final train operated, most unusually, on a Tuesday, this being an extremely rare case of a service being withdrawn in the middle of a week. One of the line's really beautiful stretches was through the Wyre Forest and the delightfully situated, and relatively isolated, Wyre Forest station is seen here on 18th March 1961. *John Langford*

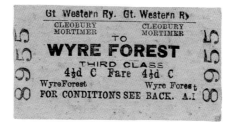

The substantial station nameboard at Woofferton Junction left passengers for Tenbury Wells and Bewdley in no doubt where they should change. The station appears to have been lovingly maintained with beautifully arranged flower beds and its attractions were enhanced by a splendid row of vintage oil lamps and an old GWR platform seat. *Stuart Ackley collection*

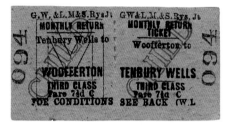

A northbound goods train, headed by an unidentified 'Hall' Class locomotive, passes through Woofferton Junction on 18th March 1961. This rural station, which was located on the main Hereford to Shrewsbury line, really does seem to have been the epitome of an English country junction but it presumably had little originating traffic and was closed from 31st July 1961 when the line to Tenbury Wells lost its passenger trains. *John Langford*

The line from Walsall to Dudley via Wednesbury Town was opened to passengers by the South Staffordshire Railway on 1st May 1850. Here, former LNWR 0-8-0 No.49361 is depicted at Walsall station while working a special train on 22nd June 1963. Walsall used to be an important traffic centre with routes fanning out in all directions but most of these lost their passenger services during the Beeching era in the 1960s. The last passenger train to Dudley ran in July 1964 while the services to Rugeley and Burton-on-Trent were withdrawn in January 1965, though it should be noted that the service to Rugeley was reinstated in 1997. *Neville Simms*

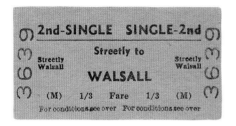

A view of the railway between Walsall station and Pleck Junction showing some of the complex and quite extensive track layout with 8F Class 2-8-0 No.48726 apparently heading towards Bescot on 14th October 1963; the lines on the far left of the picture lead to Wolverhampton. The train is passing Tasker Street goods depot which was, in effect, an extension of the former MR goods yard and depot adjacent to Walsall station. The density of traffic in the Walsall area can be gauged by the fact that Walsall shed had an allocation of 70 locomotives at its peak while in 1954 nearby Bescot shed also had an allocation of around 70 locomotives. A total of 22 of the distinctive LNWR 0-8-0s was allocated to Bescot at that time and the shed later became the last on BR to use them. *Tony Sullivan*

An industrial landscape. The former Walsall gas works provides an unappealing backdrop to this shot of tender-first Class 8F No.48680 powering a goods working towards Walsall also on 14th October 1963; this shot was taken looking southwards from the roadbridge used as a vantage point for the previous picture. The carriage sidings are just visible on the extreme left while on the opposite side of the line is the former Walsall permanent way depot. *Tony Sullivan*

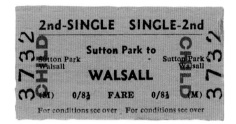

The locomotive seen in a previous picture, No.49361, was photographed on 4th May 1963 on a more mundane, everyday task working a goods train from Bescot to Walsall Midland Yard goods depot. It is seen here approaching Pleck Junction, about a mile south of Walsall station, where the line to Darlaston diverges from the 'main' line to Bescot. *Tommy Tomalin*

There were two stations serving Wednesbury, Central station on the former GWR Birmingham to Wolverhampton line and Town station on the old South Staffordshire Railway route from Walsall to Dudley. Cooling towers, pylons, chimneys and factory roofs stretch almost as far as the eye can see in this shot of former LNWR 0-8-0 No.49275 shunting south of Wednesbury Town station on 28th May 1960. The GWR line from Birmingham to Wolverhampton (Low Level) is immediately behind the photographer and the tightly curved tracks on the right, that were used solely by goods workings, connect the two routes. Note the two 'lakes' on the left of the shot – one wonders whether they attracted many bathers! In the 1959 summer timetable a total of thirteen irregular trains was provided in each direction between Walsall and Dudley, but this service was probably undermined by intensive bus competition and the route closed to passengers in 1964, as previously mentioned. The cooling towers of Ocker Hill power station form the backdrop. *R C Riley*

During the industrial revolution the town of Halesowen grew rapidly and at first the only outlet for its heavy products was a canal to Selly Oak. The Birmingham to Stourbridge line cut through high ground near Old Hill, missing Halesowen by 1½ miles, much to the frustration of the manufacturing barons. The first proposal for a railway was the ambitious Halesowen & Bromsgrove Branch Railway which was authorised in 1865, but the first line to serve the town was a branch from Old Hill, opened by the GWR on 1st March 1878. The plan to build a line to Bromsgrove was abandoned in 1870 and instead the promoters hoped to reach the MR at Northfield. The MR and GWR agreed working arrangements but by the time the company changed its name to the Halesowen Railway (HR) in 1876 there had been no progress on construction. In 1882 the line to Northfield gained Board of Trade approval and opened on 10th September 1883; in 1906 the HR was vested in the GWR and MR jointly. The Austin motor works at Longbridge, at the south end of the line, provided much of the traffic, the first siding serving the factory apparently being laid as early as 1915. Regular passenger services between Halesowen and Northfield were withdrawn as long ago as April 1919, while those northwards to Old Hill survived only a few years longer, until 5th December 1927. Workmen's trains continued to run, however, for many years afterwards, those between Old Hill and Longbridge lasting until 1st September 1958 while those linking Longbridge and Northfield survived until 4th January 1960. Halesowen was always something of a 'frontier' town with the GWR operating the line north thereof while the MR ran the line southwards to Northfield, a division of responsibilities which lasted into BR days. An interesting feature of the line was the steel trestle Dowery Dell viaduct. In this shot former GWR 0-6-0PT locomotive No.4646 is seen shunting near the former Halesowen station which was still remarkably intact at that time despite having no public passenger service for 40 years! There was a steelworks near the old station – note the tube wagon, of the type that was used to convey steel products. This photograph was taken on Saturday 10th September 1966 after the photographer visited Tyseley shed to determine what workings were in operation on that day. During week ending 12th November No.4646 was one of the last three standard gauge GWR locomotives taken out of traffic at Tyseley shed, the others being Nos.4696 and 9774. No.4646 may look dirty and neglected but it earned a place in history as one of the last descendents of an illustrious line of GWR locomotives, the history of which can be traced back to the 1830s. Three former GWR engines still survived, however, on the Aberystwyth to Devil's Bridge narrow gauge Vale of Rheidol line. *Derek Huntriss*

G. W R.

Halesowen

THE HALESOWEN BRANCH

This further picture of No.4646 shows it descending the steep, tightly-curved incline down to a canal wharf. Note the notice board instructing drivers of all goods trains to stop dead at that point, presumably to pin down brakes of loose coupled trains as necessary. This portrait was also taken on 10th September 1966. *Derek Huntriss*

A conveniently situated footbridge at Longbridge provides an ideal grandstand from where to photograph Class 2F 0-6-0 No.58271 which, assisted by sister locomotive No.58283 at the rear, was working a Birmingham area rail tour on 30th May 1959. Excited enthusiasts hurry towards the end of the platform in the hope of obtaining a quick shot before the train pulls out – the signal is 'off' and No.58271 is 'blowing off' impatiently. The footbridge linked the island platform to the Longbridge Motor Works on the right of the picture. The works, opened in 1905, has been run by various companies over the years, including the British Motor Corporation from 1952 which later became British Leyland; this was renamed the Austin Rover Group in 1982. Note that the station has none of the usual passenger facilities because it was not open to the general public, being used solely by workers from the adjacent factory. The end of each shift probably sparked a mass invasion of the platform by homegoing workers and the shelters were doubtless provided to give the large crowds a modicum of protection from the elements. *Tony Sullivan*

The Harborne Railway was conceived as a commuter route and designed to serve the fashionable western suburbs of Birmingham. It was planned as a single track branch diverging from the LNWR at Monument Lane and the GWR at Soho; it was envisaged that the line would connect with the projected Halesowen & Bromsgrove Railway. This extension was shelved together with the link with the GWR at Soho, leaving a relatively short branch just 2½ miles in length; parliamentary approval was obtained on 28th June 1866. Some years elapsed before construction got underway, perhaps because there were no local directors on the company's board, but the line eventually opened on 10th August 1874. The Harborne Railway soon became extremely popular and a money-spinner for shareholders, and the company remained independent until 1922. In its heyday it was the most profitable suburban railway in the Birmingham area and it is recorded that in 1914 it boasted no fewer than 27 trains each way, an amazingly intensive service for such a short branch line. There was even a fast lunchtime train that enabled city workers to get home for lunch! But this scenario was too good to last and in the 1920s bus competition, along a shorter and more direct route to and from the city, became intensive and the branch's fortunes declined. Main line trains on the line out of New Street had always been given priority over the branch services and this caused much delay to Harborne branch trains which did little to foster business. The line survived until the depression of the 1930s when the LMSR felt the need for economies and the Harborne branch was an obvious target, closing to passengers on 26th November 1934. Goods traffic, principally from the Chad Valley toy factory and Mitchells & Butlers brewery, continued until 4th November 1963. Not surprisingly, no pictures of the Monday to Friday branch goods trains were submitted for publication but here is Class 2F 0-6-0 No.58283 posing at Harborne with a Stephenson Locomotive Society rail tour on 30th May 1959; part of the station platform is just visible. *Tony Sullivan*

Two veteran Class 2Fs were used on this train, the other one being No.58271 which officiated at the other end of the formation. The combined ages of the two engines was 125 years, No.58271 having been constructed in 1896 while its sister locomotive was slightly younger, dating from 1897; both were built by Neilson & Co. Ltd. *Tony Sullivan*

An amazing coincidence. The Midlands Area of the Stephenson Locomotive Society was well-known for a regular programme of rail tours and on 2nd June 1962 it arranged a tour of routes in the Birmingham area using a former LNWR Class 7F 0-8-0 No.48930. The principal reason for the tour was to commemorate the centenary of the line from Aston to Sutton Coldfield which had opened exactly one hundred years previously. The line was extended from Sutton Coldfield to Lichfield in the 1880s and became a relatively busy link for Birmingham commuters. The tour halted at Gravelly Hill station and happily this stop coincided with the passage of Class 4F 0-6-0 No.44517 on a goods train. This line was not the busiest in the Birmingham area for goods traffic so the sighting of No.44517 was really quite a bonus for the participants. *Tony Sullivan*

The train depicted in the previous photograph is seen again during its stop at Sutton Coldfield. The general public appear to have totally taken over with young lads apparently enjoying the freedom of the signal box and enthusiasts unwisely walking through the very restricted space between the box and waiting locomotive. Surprisingly there is even a little girl almost standing on the track clutching the hand of a gentleman who is presumably her father – was he setting a good example? Hopefully she realised in later life that walking off platform ends is not advisable! What would one of today's health and safety officials have said about this behaviour? The goods yard at Sutton Coldfield was still busy when this shot was taken. The building on the hill in the background is the Royal Hotel. *J J Smith / Bluebell Railway Museum*

The line between Birmingham (Aston) and Lichfield was constructed on a piecemeal basis, with two separate schemes being involved, as previously mentioned. The section north of Sutton Coldfield was proposed by two local concerns both of which failed, so the LNWR came to the rescue and received powers to build the extension to Lichfield on 29th June 1880, and the route opened in 1884. There were three intermediate stations and that at Shenstone is seen in this photograph which dates from 1959. Passengers using this station benefitted from small but neat platform canopies which offered protection from the wind and rain; no expense was spared because both platforms were equipped with gentlemen's toilets. Note the very high telegraph poles that soar above the station buildings. *Lens of Sutton Association*

The 29 miles-long line from Nuneaton to Moira was opened in 1873 and was unusual in that it was constructed jointly by the LNWR and MR, a rare example of cooperation between the two rival companies; it is probably the most obscure route covered by this book. There was a triangular junction with the Leicester to Burton-on-Trent route at Moira and also a branch from Shackerstone Junction to Coalville (East) and Loughborough. It should be noted, however, that the Coalville East to Loughborough section was operated purely by the LNWR. Queen Victoria is reputed to have travelled over the Nuneaton to Moira route in 1897, her Diamond Jubilee year. Passenger services between Nuneaton and Moira were withdrawn as long ago as 12th April 1931 and even in its heyday the line had a meagre service of five trains each way daily; excursions continued, however, until the early 1960s. Passenger traffic on the Shackerstone to Loughborough branch ended on the same day. Goods traffic lingered on most of these lines until 1st July 1971 when the route was officially closed and the track, apart from a section that is operated by the Battlefield Line heritage railway, was lifted in 1973. Here, Stanier Class 8F 2-8-0 No.48216 makes a fine sight as it approaches Shackerstone station on a long southbound goods train in the early 1960s. *Tommy Tomalin*

The interesting network of lines north of Nuneaton appears to have been rarely photographed but here is a picture of Class 8F No.48644 hauling a long, empty coal train between Shackerstone Junction and Measham on 14th October 1961. The Nuneaton to Moira route and its branch towards Loughborough served many collieries and coal was doubtless its staple traffic. This route was clearly constructed as a double track line but by the time of this photograph one track had been removed. *Tommy Tomalin*

A pair of 4F Class 0-6-0s enjoy the hospitality of Overseal shed, latterly a sub-shed of Burton-on-Trent, on a sunny 14th September 1963. Overseal shed was located within the triangular junction formed where the line from Nuneaton met the Burton-on-Trent to Coalville route. Like the Nuneaton to Moira line, Overseal shed was built on a joint basis by the LNWR and MR; the latter constructed the shed building while the LNWR built the combined coal stage and tank house which can be seen on the right of the picture. The shed opened with the line in 1873 but it seems that the LNWR got the better of the deal, making much more use of the shed than the MR. Overseal shed's duties were local trip work, usually monopolised by Class 4F locomotives of the type seen here, but in the late-1950s more 8Fs started to appear in the area; however, their introduction coincided with a downturn in local goods traffic which was fast disappearing by the early 1960s. Overseal shed was closed from 6th September 1964 and a visitor in August 1965 found all of the roads lifted apart from one alongside the water column, and this little-known depot was later demolished.
Tommy Tomalin

Bearing in mind that passenger services were withdrawn between Shackerstone Junction and Loughborough (Derby Road) in 1931 it is highly unlikely that any colour pictures of regular passenger trains were ever taken on that little-known backwater. Goods traffic continued, however, and in this picture Class 4F 0-6-0 No.43861 has just arrived at the former Coalville East station with a short pick-up goods from Shepshed and is about to shunt across the extraordinary trackwork to gain entry into the granite works siding. Amazingly, the old station, which is partially visible behind the train, still appears to be reasonably intact after more than 30 years of disuse. A real gem of a photograph, portraying an everyday scene, taken at a location well off the beaten track. *Tommy Tomalin*

NUNEATON TO MOIRA AND COALVILLE (EAST)